# Foreword

I confess I am shamelessly fickle—as a reader, that is. Once, I wouldn't read anything but George Eliot, Charles Dickens, and Jane Austen, but that eventually evaporated into passionate months of Annie Dillard, Virginia Woolf, and Toni Morrison. I've gone through periods of loving mysteries, then self-help, and then, ahem, romances (scores of them in one summer!). I came late to the fantasy rage, but thanks to my good friend Carl Anderson, I'm queued up to buy the next book in the latest pseudo-medieval-dragon-magic–evil kingship series. Right now I'm in a nonfiction phase, specifically a disaster phase, where I'm morbidly reading about bubonic plagues, yellow fevers, and influenzas that have decimated humanity throughout history. I'll spare you the details, but to me it's all delightfully gross and terrifying.

What unites all my reading is a love of books and a love of *watching* myself read. I like to see how I figure out endings, navigate long, difficult passages, relate to characters, notice writing skill, react to disgusting details, and so on. In short, I enjoy being a reader as much as I enjoy reading. And that is because a few good—OK, great—teachers modeled and taught me the art of reading well. I did *not* come to school from a literate house filled with books and great literary conversations, but those *teachers* made me an under-the-covers-with-a-flashlight reader, an adult reading fanatic, reading teacher, and literacy staff developer. This is why I was delighted to receive Sarah Daunis and Maria Cassiani Iams' manuscript on making young readers healthy, strong, and smart in all their reading.

Sarah and Maria ground their foundation for fine teaching in a strong working knowledge of Bakhtin's pedagogical philosophy and

Bloom's taxonomy. They teach us about the interconnectedness of all reading genres by basing their teaching in "qualities of good reading." Defining these qualities as previewing the text and having expectations, locating oneself in the text, envisioning, inferring, and synthesizing, Sarah and Maria take us on the journey of practical implementation of teaching these qualities throughout the year.

Their method is *weekly shared reading*. Beautifully simple and profoundly powerful, weekly shared reading builds what Sarah and Maria call a "symbiotic relationship" between the teacher and the student, and most intriguing, between fluent reader and growing reader. It is their way of making visible what good readers do when they read, and then alshow to help young thinkers learn and how to make teaching "stick." What strikes me about this wonderful book is that not only do the authors tell us what they did in their classrooms, but like all good teachers, they make sure that we, the readers, know how to do what they did. At the end of this book, you will know exactly why weekly shared reading works and how to do it in your classroom.

As I read this book, I was intrigued by the questions Sarah and Maria asked themselves about their practice. Just as we want readers to ask questions as they read, we hope teachers ask questions as they teach, not questioning their students to be sure they've done their homework, but questioning the effectiveness of their own practice. One of our biggest challenges today is to give teachers the tools to reflect about their practice and to figure it out when teaching doesn't work. And while this book shows us how weekly shared reading prepares students for the omnipresent "tests," it also provides a vision for teaching that sees beyond the tests to deeply meaningful instruction that produces deeply thoughtful and proficient readers.

When I first began my fantasy-reading phase, I needed some expert fantasy readers to hold my hand until I got it. There were too many characters, too many powers in an unfamiliar world, too many enemies, and too many pages to read! But patient people stayed with me until I was willing and able to go it alone. Sometimes teachers become frustrated: it seems there is too much to teach, too many students, too many tests, and so on. Sarah and Maria understand this. But they are our weekly shared reading experts. Like my fantasy-reading friends, they will hold your hand. Their fine book will show you how to use weekly shared reading in your classroom, coach you on how to do it on your own, and then let you go to try it, play with it, and use it wisely.

And you may find that you have created some of those under-

# Text Savvy

## Using a Shared Reading Framework to Build Comprehension

GRADES 3-6

**Sarah Daunis**
**Maria Cassiani Iams**

FOREWORD BY
Janet Angelillo

HEINEMANN
Portsmouth, NH

**Heinemann**
361 Hanover Street
Portsmouth, NH 03801–3912
www.heinemann.com

*Offices and agents throughout the world*

**Library of Congress Cataloging-in-Publication Data**
Daunis, Sarah.
    Text savvy : using a shared reading framework to build comprehension,
grades 3–6 / Sarah Daunis and Maria Cassiani Iams.
        p. cm.
    Includes bibliographical references.
    ISBN-13: 978-0-325-01002-1
    ISBN-10: 0-325-01002-1
    1. Reading (Elementary).  2. Reading comprehension.  I. Iams, Maria
Cassiani.  II. Title.
LB1573.D268 2007
372.47—dc22                                                2007009345

*Editor:* Kerry Herlihy and Kate Montgomery
*Production:* Lynne Costa
*Cover design:* Jenny Jensen Greenleaf
*Cover illustrations:* © Corbis
*Typesetter:* Valerie Levy / Drawing Board Studios
*Manufacturing:* Jamie Carter

Printed in the United States of America on acid-free paper
11  10  09  08      RRD      2  3  4  5

*To our mentors—Janet Angelillo, Adele Schroeter, and Leslie Zackman—*
*for inspiring us, and to our husbands—*
*Matt Ransford and Michael Iams—for encouraging us.*

SDRD and MCI

# Contents

the-covers-with-a-flashlight, passionate readers we all dream about birthing. With Sarah and Maria, let us recognize this as our work and teach so wisely that we give it as our gift to the world.

—*Janet Angelillo*

# Acknowledgments

Just as we impact our students' lives and they ours, many mentors, leaders, and guides have influenced our teaching and learning and have helped us grow up as practitioners.

The Teachers College Reading and Writing Project set the stage for our growth as educators, and we are indebted to Lucy Calkins for her vision, commitment, and practice in reading and writing instruction. Whether it was while reading one of Lucy's books, watching her present at a Calendar Day, having the good fortune of shadowing her in our classrooms, or being a student in her graduate class at Teachers College, our thinking and instruction were transformed by her insight.

Janet Angellilo supported us as a staff developer and as a mentor. As a staff developer, her expert demonstration of best practices in writing workshop defined our writing instruction—from meaningful punctuation and revision work to purposeful writing about reading. As a mentor, she encouraged us to pursue professional inquiry, write about our thinking, and channel our energy into a book. Her faith in our abilities was both humbling and invigorating.

Lucy's team of staff developers further encouraged us to rethink our teaching, try new practices, and incorporate reflection into our craft. Christine Lagatta worked with us for two years, helping us fine-tune our pedagogy and deepen our content knowledge. Cory Gillette's wisdom impacted how we facilitated conversations in our classroom, placing rightful ownership of the learning on the students. Our foundational knowledge about emergent and early readers and writers grew tremendously with the guidance and mastery of our primary-grade staff developer, Shanna Schwartz. We were most fortunate to work side by side with Mary Chiarella, who further affected our literacy instruction on a daily basis. And finally, our thinking was altered and our instruction improved through Leadership Groups led by Janet Angelillo, Coleen Cruz, and Jessica Fairbanks, and through Calendar Days at Teachers College, where we hung onto every word that Carl Anderson, Kathleen Tolan, Randy Bomer, Maggie Moon, Dorothy Barnhouse, Cheryl Tyler, and many others so wisely said.

PS59 in Manhattan is a true learning community, led by wise educators, supported by smart teachers, and abundant with fabulously diverse students. Strengthened by its partnership with The Reading and Writing Project at Teachers College, PS59 is a place where professional inquiry is encouraged and sustained.

Our instructional leadership team, composed of our principal, Adele Schroeter, and our instructional superintendent, Leslie Zackman, were literacy coaches and experts in their own right. Authors, teachers, and leaders, Adele and Leslie knew and understood best practices in literacy instruction and possessed a wealth of literacy content knowledge. Furthermore, Adele and Leslie supported and encouraged professional inquiry. To that end, they ensured that teachers had common planning times and vast opportunities to attend professional development both on-site and off-site. The conversation about effective teaching practices never ended, but was continuously facilitated by our leadership team. To Adele and Leslie, we are most grateful and thankful.

We are also honored by the guidance of Anna Marie Carrillo, our instructional superintendent during our last year at PS59. Her sharp eye for best practices and purposeful instruction and her commitment to immediate and constructive feedback further developed our craft.

To our upper-grade colleagues, we express our thanks and gratitude for their willingness to take on a new initiative, weekly shared reading, and own it. Wendy Binkowitz, Jennifer Chalfin, Jennifer Lui, and Barbara Rossi let us try out our thinking in their classrooms and then implemented weekly shared reading with our support. Their stories grace these pages, and it was our great pleasure to work and learn alongside them.

Thanks to Karen Fishbein, Lianne Nestler, and Anastasia Macris for also taking on the work in their classrooms. A special thanks to Connie Wu, who helped us gather texts for weekly shared reading.

Even though we are upper-elementary-grade teachers, we have grown up around the smart work of our primary staff. We have learned so much from Danielle Apicella, Annie Bochner, Destiny Braddick, Jung Choe, Trina Dremel, Cheryl Leisyengang, Andrea Mackoff, Stephanie Nichols, Katherine Nigen, Lindsey Powell, and

Heather Tripp. And thank you to Alina Durso, whose thinking greatly affected upper-grade instruction.

Thank you to Ruth Flaschner, who indulged us when we requested substitutes and schedule changes so that we could grow professionally both outside and inside the building, and reminded us to take care of ourselves when we left school late at night.

We began our journey as educators before we taught at PS59, and our mentors, colleagues, and teammates have influenced us greatly: Rob Meehan, Lynn Kelly, Mark Reidel, Terry Romer, Tom Balakas, Darin Carney, and Marcee Kutner, from Cherry Creek Schools in Englewood, Colorado; Kathy Collins and Jessica Borg, from PS321 in Brooklyn, New York; Britt Hamre and Celia Oyler, from Teachers College; Katie Altschule, Hannah Chandler, Shannon Lamb, Dawn Selnes, and Kristina Sullivan; and the many others who helped us on our way.

We also acknowledge the people at The Wheeler School and in Denver Public Schools for providing us with new opportunities for professional growth.

What began as a professional inquiry turned into a book proposal, which then was expertly crafted into a book by our editor, Kerry Herlihy, whose encouragement, suggestions, and input were most appreciated. Melissa Wood nad Lynne Costa organized the pieces of *Text Savvy*, and Kate Montgomery launched us into authorship. We are humbled by their commitment to our professional growth, and we literally could not have done this without their guidance and support.

We thank the people in our lives who have watched us grow up and have been our biggest fans for quite some time. We honor our parents as our first teachers—excellent teachers. Thank you, Alex and Diana Daunis and John and Erena Cassiani. We are grateful for the encouragement and love from our sisters and brothers-in-law—thank you, Julia Daunis, Amanda Daunis, Gina Cassiani Hutchins, Scott Dvorin, and Carl Hutchins. We appreciate our husbands' patience and understanding as we monopolized the computer, talked on the phone all night, or disappeared at dinnertime for hours. Matt Ransford and Michael Iams, your support is invaluable. We thanks our dear friends as well.

Lastly, we acknowledge the students who have watched us grow up as teachers in their classrooms. It was their thinking, their challenges, and their successes that probed our thinking and changed our instruction. Every student makes an impact on us as teachers and pushes us to grow as learners. So thank you to the students in our past and the students in our future, for your contribution to our growth as practitioners.

# Introduction

[The word] becomes "one's own" only when the speaker populates it with his own intention, his own accent, when he appropriates the word, adapting it to his own semantic and expressive intention. Prior to this moment of appropriation the word . . . exists in other people's mouths, in other people's contexts, serving other people's intentions; it is from there that one must take the word, and make it one's own.

—MIKHAIL BAKHTIN, *The Dialogic Imagination: Four Essays*

## Skills Without Borders

Every year, I taught a variety of units of study. In November, the students became experts at nonfiction reading; in April, the students learned reading strategies to tackle poetry.[1] We delved deeply into each unit, focusing all of our attention on the skills readers needed *in order to be successful in that genre*. In some way, we treated each unit as a separate entity, somehow forgetting to highlight those overarching qualities of good reading that we returned to with each unit of study. I now realize that *I* treated most units as a new journey,

---

[1] While we have chosen, for continuity, to write in the first person, we created weekly shared reading together. This book grew out of our shared experiences—Maria's experiences as a third- and fourth-grade teacher and as a literacy coach, and Sarah's experiences as a fourth- and fifth-grade teacher.

instead of making it overtly clear that *there were certain skills that a reader utilized regardless of the genre.*

In reality, there were *five essential reading skills*[2] that I returned to repeatedly:

- previewing the text and having expectations
- locating oneself in the text
- envisioning
- inferring
- synthesizing

I realize that I had not made it abundantly clear to my students that regardless of the unit, these were overarching skills that readers should always employ to fully understand the text. Instead, I had inadvertently encouraged my students to compartmentalize their learning—they kept their fluency *within* each unit of study.

It was not as if my kids weren't mastering the skills taught within a unit. The question was: Why they weren't bringing their prior knowledge to the next unit of study? Why weren't they inherently using what they had already been taught? Why weren't they building skills upon skills from unit to unit? I realized, as Bakhtin so clearly states in the epigraph, that these skills existed "in other people's mouths, in other people's contexts, serving other people's intentions." I had to figure out how to give my students ownership of their learning, how to "make it one's own."

# Structures in Place

As an upper-elementary-grade teacher,[3] I had a number of structures in place in order to effectively support my students as readers. My

---

[2] Depending on the author or educator, the terms *skills* or *strategies* are used to describe readers' thinking while reading. Here, we are using the term *skills*, based on the Teachers College Reading and Writing Project's definition of reading skills (e.g., synthesizing), and reading strategies (e.g., asking yourself, "What is this page mostly about?"). Proficient readers employ these five reading skills to make meaning and deepen their comprehension of the text.

[3] In reference to grades three through six.

students developed their reading skills within a balanced literacy model—through minilessons, small-group work, read-alouds, shared reading, and individualized conferences.

With minilessons, I demonstrated one clear teaching point; minilessons were designed to help my students successfully navigate our current reading unit of study. Each lesson built upon the previous one; I drew from conversations from the days before and anticipated what reading strategies the students would need to more successfully read a specific genre. The beauty of the minilesson format was that it provided my students with the opportunity to try it; they were given a chance to immediately approximate the reading strategy, skill, or behavior that was just introduced to them. Small-group instruction enabled me to teach or reteach an appropriate and needed strategy to a specific group of students. The instruction was purposefully targeted for the three or four students who sat with me. During read-alouds, I was able to model the habits of a successful reader. I was able to introduce ways to respond to or interact with the text. I could revisit skills that the whole class was still struggling with or preview a new strategy that I would return to during a minilesson. During shared reading instruction, I was able to reinforce fluency, expression, and word-attack strategies. I could return to the shared reading texts as students refined their meaning-making strategies—strategies that students could begin to use independently with new texts. And finally, in individual conferences, I complimented my students for taking on a strategy and using it proficiently, and then taught them a strategy or skill that would allow them to delve deeper into their texts.

With each of these structures—minilessons, small-group work, read-alouds, shared reading, and conferring—the students were introduced to a variety of strategies that could be incorporated into their toolbox of reading skills. These were powerful structures, designed to strengthen their reading skills, to ensure deep comprehension, and to move them toward independence.

Yet, as I taught third, fourth, and fifth grades, I noticed that from unit of study to unit of study, and more disconcerting, from year to year, students needed "refresher courses" when reactivating particular reading skills. Their tenuous understanding and oftentimes limited use of such skills throughout the year made it difficult for them to deepen their reading comprehension or to take on these skills *as their own.* While the work students did became somewhat deeper from unit to unit and year to year, I found that there was this feeling that I was starting from scratch whenever I began a new reading unit.

With this in mind, I realized that there needed to be a consistent, explicit structure in place, a structure that could enable students to practice *all* of their reading strategies *regardless of the current unit of study. Weekly shared reading* was created in response.

# Weekly Shared Reading

Weekly shared reading is a ten- to fifteen-minute structure that takes place outside of reading workshop. It is designed to highlight the aforementioned five essential reading skills on a weekly basis. Unlike minilessons, where the students are taught and asked to briefly try out a new strategy *related* to the current unit of study, weekly shared reading is a five-day model where kids repeatedly return to those five essential reading skills *regardless* of the current unit of study.

Each week, the teacher selects (in response to the identified needs of the students) a text from a different genre. The class stays with this same text for the entire week, but focuses on one of the top five skills each day. (Over the course of a month, a teacher might pick a poem for week one, a nonfiction article for week two, a realistic fiction story for week three, and a primary source document for week four.) Week after week, the students return to this five-day model. Students are encouraged to flex their reading muscles with a variety of genres.

With this repeated five-day model, the students can anticipate what skill they'll be focusing on—they know what we do each day ("On Mondays, we . . . On Tuesdays, we . . ."). Unlike minilessons, where the students are *taught to* use a strategy, the explicit and repetitive nature of this structure encourages the students to take ownership of this shared conversation. The power of this model is that it allows the teacher and students to cocreate meaning. Karen Gallas (1995) in *Talking Their Way into Science: Hearing Children's Questions and Theories, Responding with Curricula*, outlines the benefits of allowing students the opportunity to "co-construct, or build together, ideas about seminal questions through real dialogue"(11). She elaborates:

> A closer examination of what happened when children were allowed to collaborate in their thinking without my interference showed me that the process of collaboration had great potential to teach *me* about children's thinking . . . It was as if the eavesdropping I spoke of earlier became formalized, and I could view how their ideas developed, watched theories being built, and be amazed at the power of a group of children thinking together. (12)

Alongside the benefit of coconstructing meaning, this model provides the teacher with immediate access to student thinking. Finding opportunities to access student thinking is key because it sheds light on the effectiveness of one's own teaching. While turn-and-talks and one-on-one conferences give me a sense of what the children have grasped and what I need to reteach, I find that it's challenging to get to all of my students in a timely fashion. In response to this dilemma, Christine Lagatta, a staff developer for the Teachers College Reading and Writing Project, introduced me to the idea of *assessing on the run*, a flexible structure that allows me to note a great number of students' strengths and needs within a communal setting. With assessing on the run, I teach a handful of kids a strategy and have them immediately try it. I am then able to quickly assess who understands and who needs more support. Assessing on the run nicely dovetails with weekly shared reading, as that structure provides me with another opportunity to efficiently and effectively assess my students as readers as I move them toward independence.

# Pushing Readers in Upper-Elementary Classrooms

In *Text Savvy: Using a Shared Reading Framework to Build Comprehension, Grades 3–6*, I explain how weekly shared reading supports readers in the upper-elementary grades. I use anecdotes and examples from the field to enhance teachers' understanding of how to implement this model in the classroom and use weekly shared reading assessment as a way to better inform and plan minilessons, conferences, small-group work, and future weekly shared reading instruction. I also describe how this structure

- benefits students by letting them practice with a fluent reader
- allows for a public demonstration of kids' reading skills
- shows students how proficient readers consistently integrate five essential reading skills in order to understand a variety of texts in a variety of genres
- allows additional time for assessment, detailing the power and possibilities of assessing on the run
- supports the wide range of readers in a classroom
- supports students in test preparation and in other curricular areas
- grew out of and impacted the supportive PS59 teaching and learning community

# Final Thoughts

Weekly shared reading provided my students with an opportunity to take ownership of their learning. This model encouraged students to cocreate meaning—to take part in the instruction. Furthermore, by repeatedly returning to the five essential reading skills, I no longer felt as if I was starting from scratch. I was able to provide my students with a scaffolded structure that bridged the gap between teacher-led instruction and student independence.

# A Structure of Support for Upper-Grade Readers

1

## Camilla and Evan

Late in the day on a May afternoon, I found myself enthralled by the recent published poetry writing of my fifth-grade students. Camilla, a student who had previously struggled with her writing, was able to evoke the poetry of Langston Hughes as she wrote about how difficult life can be. Evan's deep comprehension of poems and use of imagery in his writing clearly grew out of the class' daily discussions.

My students' poetry far surpassed—in quality and depth—the stories, literary essays, and personal narratives that they had published over the course of the school year. Although I had used the same craft strategies, introduced them to relevant touchstone texts, and provided them with a rigorous workshop model, their poetry writing clearly stood out among their other fiction and nonfiction pieces. I asked myself what made this unit so unique. What could I do to ensure that my students had the same level of success with all of our units of study?

## The Birth of Weekly Shared Reading

As I reflected on the work that we had done in the course of the school year, it occurred to me that the fundamental difference between my students' solid knowledge of poetry and their familiarity with the other genres stemmed from the fact that we had read, discussed, analyzed, acted out, and responded with drawings to the *poem of the week* every day since the first week of school (as Georgia Heard [1999] recommends in *Awakening the Heart*). For ten to fifteen minutes every afternoon, in addition to reading workshop, the students strengthened their reading skills as the class cocreated a shared language about and understanding of poetry.

By the time I had launched reading and writing poetry units of study in April, the students had been exposed to, reflected on, and analyzed more than thirty poems. Embedding a poem of the week into my fifth-grade curriculum provided my students with additional opportunities to practice the reading skills and strategies introduced during reading minilessons. The students developed a heightened fluency in, appreciation for, and understanding of the poetry genre.

Armed with this knowledge, I realized that if I could continue to provide the experience of having additional time to practice reading strategies and build reading skills, but vary it among different genres, I would be able to provide my students with opportunities to engage in deeper conversations about a variety of genres and further strengthen their abilities as readers. The following September, I implemented weekly shared reading in my fifth-grade classroom.

# The Existing Structure of Shared Reading in Balanced Literacy Classrooms

In primary-grade classrooms, shared reading often reinforces fluency, expression, and word-attack strategies for emergent and early readers. Teachers return to texts over and over again so that students can refine their meaning-making strategies—strategies that students can begin to use independently in new texts.

As students become more proficient and fluent readers, their reading patterns change; they are more likely to activate prior knowledge, make more connections between themselves and texts, and understand various points of view (Brown 2004). However, Brown asserts that

> [teachers] often assume that because their students can read, they do not have to be taught reading skills . . . problems arise when teachers do not recognize that their older students may still need instruction in reading complex texts or understanding on a more sophisticated level. (7)

Shared reading, an element of balanced literacy, is a collaborative learning activity where teachers of all grade levels effectively and consistently model reading skills, strategies, and behaviors and engage students in their use (Holdaway 1980; Parkes 2000; Routman 2000; Brown 2004). The significant feature of shared reading is the cooperative meaning making of the text between readers and listeners. While the read-aloud serves as the "to" (teacher reads to students), and the independent work serves as the "by" (reading is done by students), the collaborative work in shared reading is the "with" (teacher reads with students). This *gradual release of responsibility*, from the "to" to the "by," represents the shift that occurs when the responsibility for learning moves from the teacher to the student (Pearson and Gallagher 1983). In shared reading, the teacher initially provides the support by reading the text out loud and modeling specific strategies; gradually, however, he encourages the students to contribute their ideas in making meaning of the text together (Brown 2004). The shared reading structure forms a bridge between teacher-led learning and independent application.

Shared reading of more complex texts in the upper grades allows for more sophisticated discussions about the text, while concurrently offering entry points for all learners in the classroom. Because the teacher reads the text aloud to the students, the students' thinking work can go beyond decoding the text with phrasing and fluency. In addition to modeling a fluent reading of a more complicated text, the teacher also models a specific reading strategy—and the integration of that reading strategy with the other reading strategies good readers use all the time. The teacher shares her thinking work and encourages students to think along with her. Students strengthen their reading strategy application, their thinking and ideas about the text, their conversation about the text, and their content knowledge with the guidance of an expert reader and thinker. As Brown states,

"Shared reading can be used to simultaneously unlock the meaning in a text and teach the integration and application of strategies that students can apply to the next piece of text" (2004, 13).

Brenda Parkes' (2000) *Read It Again! Revisiting Shared Reading* helps teachers rethink the power and possibilities of shared reading instruction. Her book, focusing on primary-grade classrooms, suggests that shared reading has two purposes: to provide children with an enjoyable reading experience, enticing them to become readers themselves, and to explicitly teach students how to be readers and writers themselves. Students are engaged in applying reading strategies, skills, and behaviors to a familiar text that the entire class experiences. With emergent and early readers, the foci of shared reading are often word work and fluency, such as recognizing high-frequency words in books and using the patterns in books to read with phrasing and fluency. In our kindergarten classrooms, teachers spend a portion of their morning meeting with shared reading texts. The teacher and students often read two or three shared texts during their morning gathering. Often, teachers utilize the same text many times; each time, the purpose of shared reading varies.

While Parkes focuses on shared reading in the primary grades, her thinking about shared reading has powerful implications for readers at any level. Readers vary the way they read according to their purpose and the type of text. Parkes reminds us that

> each text type has its own characteristics and makes its own demands of readers. Becoming familiar with these characteristics gives readers a powerful source of prediction. This in turn supports rapid processing of text and fluency. Shared reading is a perfect vehicle for introducing and involving children in a range of text types. (2000, 70)

In my fifth-grade classroom, I used—and still use—the structure of shared reading in various minilessons within units of study. Having all eyes on one text is a powerful teaching and learning opportunity. Because I use the overhead, I can watch my students' level of engagement and understanding during a shared reading; their eyes are on the text while my eyes are on the overhead and them.

It wasn't until I witnessed my students' deep understanding of poems that I realized I could use the powerful structure of shared reading *outside* of the reading workshop—at another point in the day, as another opportunity for modeling and practice. Much like the primary students, who often engage in shared reading inside and outside of the reading workshop, my upper-grade students were going to do the same.

# Building Upon Heard's Poem of the Week

As I developed weekly shared reading, I thought back to Georgia Heard's (1999) five-day structure for the poem of the week, and mimicked it, understanding the value of repeatedly returning to a text and growing our understanding about it. Georgia Heard's approach to poetry immersion suggests that students and teachers spend a week with a poem. Every day, an understanding of the poem develops because students and teachers revisit it in a shared reading structure.

*Overview of the Poem of the Week Structure*\*

Day One: The teacher reads the poem with the class; the teacher and class begin to discuss its meaning.

Day Two: The students draw the images that come to mind as they read and hear the poem.

Day Three: The students act out the poem, either within a small group or in front of the whole class.

Day Four: The class further analyzes the poem by making personal corrections to the poem.

Day Five: The class says good-bye to the poem, and students and teachers offer each other final thoughts and feelings about this week's celebrated poem.

Heard sets up a scaffold, or support, for students and teachers as they grow their understanding about the poem of the week. The class engages in thinking work that becomes more complex as the week progresses. By building a strong foundation at the beginning of the

---

\*Paraphrased by the authors.

week, with repeated readings of the poem, the class can analyze it and come to a deeper understanding of it by the end of the week.

## Building Upon Bloom's Taxonomy

As I fine-tuned the construct of weekly shared reading, I thought about Bloom's taxonomy; I wanted to secure students' foundational understanding of a text *prior* to encouraging them to infer or synthesize information from the text. Fifty years ago, Benjamin Bloom (1956) developed a classification of levels of behavior important for learning. The levels range on a continuum from the simplest behaviors to the most complex:

- Knowledge: observe and recall information
- Comprehension: understand information; grasp meaning
- Application: use information or methods in new situations
- Analysis: recognize patterns and identify components
- Synthesis: generalize from given facts; relate knowledge from several areas; use old ideas to create new ones
- Evaluation: compare and discriminate between ideas; make judgments about information

Bloom asserts that learners must master a level before proceeding to the next. However, throughout the school day, learners are presented tasks that require them to engage in the entire range of learning behaviors. Some students may become frustrated when asked to synthesize or evaluate a text when they don't comprehend it initially. With this in mind, I organized weekly shared reading to engage students in the more simple learning behaviors first *before* moving to the more sophisticated and complex learning behaviors.

## Considering Cambourne's Conditions for Learning

As a smart and caring classroom teacher, I felt like I provided a safe, nurturing, and academically rigorous environment for all of my students. However, upon reexamining Brian Cambourne's (1988) conditions for learning, I realized that I could further create the conditions for learning in reading by implementing weekly shared reading in the classroom. Brian Cambourne asserts that children tend to learn most effectively when eight essential conditions exist in learning environments.

Table 1    The Conditions for Learning in Reading and Writing*

| Condition | Teaching and Learning Implications | How It's Developed Through Weekly Shared Reading |
|---|---|---|
| Immersion | *Immerse learners in a wide range of texts in all genres (poetry, biography, fiction, nonfiction).* | Throughout a month, readers are immersed in four different texts within four varying genres. |
| Demonstration | *Learners need to see many demonstrations in meaningful contexts of the skills and strategies fluent readers and writers use.* | The teacher supports reading skill and strategy development by modeling fluent reading behaviors. |
| Expectation | *Children are more likely to engage in the demonstrations of people close to them, who hold high expectations for them and who have confidence in their ability to succeed.* | The teacher expects all students to participate and contribute in shared reading instructional time. The teacher expects that students' abilities will grow through more practice. |
| Responsibility | *Learners must assume responsibility for learning, which includes having opportunities to make decisions regarding that learning.* | As the school year progresses, the students assume more responsibility for the conversation during weekly shared reading. |
| Practice | *Learners need time and opportunity to use and practice their developing skills in meaningful ways.* | Weekly shared reading offers students opportunities to practice their reading skills in a supportive environment. |
| Approximation | *Children need to feel safe taking risks while practicing what they are taught and know that their approximations will be accepted, guided, and encouraged.* | Students practice their developing reading skills together, in a safe and encouraging environment. |
| Response | *Feedback is an essential part of learning. New learners need to feel their efforts are valued. Learners need to be encouraged to take responsibility for their learning.* | The teacher responds to students' needs by quickly assessing students and providing supportive instruction, validating students' efforts. |
| Engagement | *Children need to actively engage if learning is to take place. This condition is essential.* | Weekly shared reading encourages engagement from all learners, regardless of reading strengths and behaviors. Multiple entry points are provided for learners throughout the week, and the teacher supports learners as they practice reading skills and strategies. |

* Adapted by New York City Department of Education from the work of Brian Cambourne.

# The Structure of Weekly Shared Reading

Keeping consistent with Heard's ten- to fifteen-minute time frame for the poem of the week, building upon Bloom's idea of scaffolded instruction, and maximizing Cambourne's conditions for learning in reading, weekly shared reading became part of the upper-grade curriculum at PS59. The drastic difference in my students' understanding of poetry was quite convincing that more practice with sophisticated texts was necessary for upper-grade readers as they strengthened and solidified their reading skills. After recognizing the five essential reading skills (further explained in Chapter 2) that proficient readers integrate while reading, I set up a five-day systematic way to discuss texts within and across genres. The cyclical structure of weekly shared reading enabled me to provide sufficient time for students to practice a variety of reading strategies in a supportive environment, to assess students' reading skills, and to plan for future instruction.

Alongside my reading and writing workshops, weekly shared reading became valued as an important part of my day. From the get-go, I explained to my students that this added structure would allow us to slow things down, to take the time to join in a shared conversation, to think deeply about a handful of texts. Since my students were already familiar with the idea of a mentor text, this new structure was not that foreign to them. While the idea of staying with a text five days and looking at it in five different ways was new, the foundation of our classroom community was one that valued thinking deeply about our reading and writing work. Therefore, weekly shared reading perfectly supported those goals and was readily accepted by my students.

## A Week at a Glance

During the week, I focus on one of the five essential reading skills each day, modeling a very specific reading strategy to build that skill. Every week, I focus on the same five reading skills; the reading strategies modeled and practiced vary from week to week.

Table 2   Weekly Shared Reading: A Week at a Glance

| Day of Week | Reading Skill | Examples of Reading Strategies That Support the Skill |
|---|---|---|
| Monday<br><br>*Having a First Glance* | Previewing the text and having expectations | • previewing text<br>• scanning page and pointing out features<br>• defining genre<br>• confirming genre after text is read<br>• setting expectations for the text<br>• setting a purpose for reading |
| Tuesday<br><br>*Doing a Double Take* | Locating oneself in the text | • thinking, "What do I know about this topic already?"<br>• thinking, "What might be new information for me?"<br>• explaining, "These connections help me understand the text because . . ."<br>• explaining, "These questions help me understand the text because . . ."<br>• reading and thinking, "What is the text mostly about?"<br>• reading and thinking, "What information is important and what information is interesting?" |
| Wednesday<br><br>*Filling in the Picture* | Envisioning | • creating a movie in your mind<br>• thinking about what you see in your mind's eye<br>• creating graphic organizers you can see in your head<br>• reading and "filing" information<br>• sketching a picture or diagram |
| Thursday<br><br>*Digging Deeper* | Inferring | • thinking about the big ideas in a text<br>• thinking about the moral or lesson of a story<br>• paying close attention while reading to detect the author's tone and slant<br>• identifying the author's perspective |
| Friday<br><br>*Getting the Big Picture* | Synthesizing | • reading and thinking, "What do I know *now* about this topic? Where is the evidence to support my thinking?"<br>• reading and thinking, "How has my thinking changed? How have I revised my thinking?"<br>• stating what the text is mostly about<br>• having ideas about the text as a whole<br>• preparing for accountable conversation |

Table 3    The Structure of Weekly Shared Reading

| | |
|---|---|
| **What the Students Are Doing** | • sitting on the rug in the meeting area next to their reading partners<br>• looking at text on the overhead (or enlarged text)<br>• listening as the teacher reads the text out loud<br>• listening as the teacher models and encourages use of specific strategies to build essential reading skills<br>• practicing reading strategies with the enlarged text<br>• turning to talk to their reading partners |
| **What the Teacher Is Doing** | • modeling the habits and behaviors of a fluent reader<br>• identifying one or two aspects of the text that support the strategy being taught<br>• encouraging students to practice the strategy with her<br>• assessing on the run<br>• listening in on partnership conversation |
| **Materials/Time Frame** | • 10–15 minutes per day, five days a week<br>• teacher-selected texts in a variety of genres—enlarged or on the overhead<br>• shared reading text is copied for students and placed in weekly shared reading folders, so students can refer to the text and use it as a resource<br>• in fifth grade, students use a shared reading notebook to jot down their thinking before, during, and after weekly shared reading<br>• anecdotal notes for assessing on the run |

The content of weekly shared reading focuses on teaching and practicing reading strategies to build the five essential reading skills that proficient readers consistently utilize. The structure of weekly shared reading follows the existing and comfortable structure of any shared reading instruction.

## Text Selection for Weekly Shared Reading

As I plan for weekly shared reading in my classroom, I am committed to providing opportunities to practice reading strategies and build reading skills with a variety of genres. At the beginning of the school year, when I don't know my readers as well, I set up a monthly cycle of nonfiction, fiction, poetry, and "other." The other consists of the more unique genres of text, such as menus, maps, charts or tables, and flyers. As I get to know my readers, my monthly cycle of shared reading text might change, based on my readers' needs. Different from mentor texts that are used during reading and writing workshops to highlight a genre-specific technique within a unit of study, these texts are designed to push the boundaries of a reading unit of study. I pick texts based on the overarching needs of my students *as readers.* In planning weekly shared reading with third-grade colleagues, our assessment of the students revealed that our third graders needed more reading skill and strategy practice on short narrative and nonnarrative nonfiction. The "other" during a few monthly cycles became another nonfiction text in an effort to support these third-grade readers.

As I model the strategies of a proficient reader, I remind students that I often go back to my favorite books again and again. I talk about how I pick up on details previously unnoticed or how I deepen my understanding of myself with each reread. Furthermore, I model the value of returning to a text when I do not understand, demonstrating how important it is to make sense of my reading. Therefore, it has been very easy for my students to understand why I would pick one text and stick with it for the entire week—my students know that smart readers can and should return to the same text again and again.

I find the short texts for weekly shared reading in various places —pages from the books in my classroom, snippets of magazine articles, and even good test-preparation materials. I select a text that is either on or slightly above the average reading level in my classroom; because I'm the one doing the fluent reading of the text, my students can engage in the meaning making and thinking. Regardless, the texts I use during weekly shared reading mimic the more sophisticated texts that my upper-grade readers encounter throughout the school year.

Before I just slap a shared text on the overhead, I really examine it and think about it. Depending on the strategies I want to highlight, a potential short text may or may not be the most ideal one to use in weekly shared reading. Just as I am thoughtful about the read-aloud books I choose, I am also thoughtful and purposeful about the weekly shared reading texts I present.

# Ongoing Reflection

The consistency of weekly shared reading's five-day model allows my students to safely test the waters, to comfortably push their boundaries of understanding. Initially, I provide support by reading the text out loud and modeling specific strategies; gradually, however, I encourage the students to contribute their ideas in making meaning of the text together (Brown 2004). The process is thoughtful and somewhat fluid—designed in response to the needs of my students. Just as I needed to stand on the shoulders of Georgia Heard, Benjamin Bloom, and Brian Cambourne, weekly shared reading allows my students to stand onto my shoulders, to have a better understanding of what it looks and feels like to be a proficient reader.

# Big Ideas from Chapter 1

- Every week of weekly shared reading follows the same skill focus.
- Monday's skill is previewing the text and having expectations.
- Tuesday's skill is locating oneself in the text.
- Wednesday's skill is envisioning.
- Thursday's skill is inferring.
- Friday's skill is synthesizing.
- Teachers focus on specific reading strategies based on students' needs.
- Teachers choose weekly shared reading texts based on students' needs.

# *Five Essential Reading Skills Used by Proficient Readers*

**2**

**Tringa**

Tringa, a fifth grader, came into my classroom reading on grade level—a solid 3, according to the state reading assessment rubric, a proficient reader. She was a committed student, always wanting to do her best. She read a wide variety of texts over extended periods of time. She tried all of the strategies introduced in class, yet continued to retain a very literal interpretation of the texts she read.

Tringa spoke English as her second language and did not have someone who modeled fluent reading of English at home. As she encountered more sophisticated texts, I knew that she would need extra support.

I wondered how I could support Tringa on two levels: How could I push this literal reader to infer big ideas beyond the text, moving her from one who met the standards to one who exceeded them? And how could I ensure that Tringa maintained comprehension as she encountered new vocabulary? In short, how could I nudge her from a 3 to a 4?

Teaching kids how to read with meaning and understanding often prompts me to examine the work I do as a fluent and skillful reader. I switch from reading one genre to another within minutes; over the course of a day, I read memos, newspapers, articles, professional texts, fiction novels, menus, and grocery lists. And I read all texts successfully, with full comprehension. So what is it that I do as a proficient reader that allows me to understand a range of text genres?

While I do employ genre-specific reading strategies to understand the appropriate text, I consistently utilize a number of reading skills, no matter what I'm reading. I've thought of these as the five essential reading skills that help me understand any text.

# Five Essential Reading Skills

As mentioned in the Introduction, the five essential reading skills proficient readers consistently use are as follows:

- previewing the text and having expectations
- locating oneself in the text
- envisioning
- inferring
- synthesizing

The integration of the five essential reading skills allows readers to understand the text, interact with the text, and own, or be able to effectively talk about, the text. Ellin Oliver Keene and Susan Zimmermann (1997) refer to this integration as a *mosaic*. In their book *Mosaic of Thought: Teaching Comprehension in a Reader's Workshop*, Keene and Zimmermann highlight seven reading strategies that deepen comprehension: activating prior knowledge, determining importance, questioning, using visual/sensory images, inferring, retelling/synthesizing, and using fix-up strategies. The five essential reading skills I find proficient readers use are based not only on this work but also on the thinking from *Strategies That Work: Teaching Comprehension to Enhance Understanding*, in which Stephanie Harvey and Anne Goudvis (2000) demonstrate that when readers make connections, question, infer, determine importance, visualize, synthesize, and monitor for meaning, they have a fuller and more complete understanding of the text.

I want my students to consistently employ these reading skills to understand any text, as I do in my adult reading life. However, I've noticed that as my upper-grade students encounter more sophisticated texts, they seem to abandon the very fundamental reading habits, skills, and strategies that will enable them to comprehend the material. I've watched students who I thought were strong readers go from understanding a realistic fiction text to struggling through a historical fiction text on the same reading level. I've seen some students devour nonfiction science articles only to watch their eyes glaze over when they attempt to read and understand poetry. As I reflected on this disconnect, I realized that while I taught my kids genre-specific reading skills and strategies within a unit of study, I too had abandoned teaching and modeling the fundamental reading skills that proficient readers consistently utilize. No wonder my young students couldn't sustain the use of these reading skills—I wasn't providing enough practice. That's why I created a structure that allows me to highlight the five essential reading skills and allows my students to consistently practice them, infusing them into their reading lives. Weekly shared reading grants weekly attention to each of the five essential reading skills.

# A Closer Look at the Essential Skills

Within every unit of study in reading, I model a range of reading strategies, showing students how I can build the reading skills that allow me to understand a text. While the following reading skills are taught through minilessons in my reading workshop, I explicitly reteach them during weekly shared reading.

## Having a First Glance: Previewing the Text and Having Expectations

When proficient readers are about to read a text, they quickly identify the genre of the text and, therefore, have expectations of the text. This prereading skill—also considered a behavior—happens so quickly that skilled readers might not even realize they do it. Randy Bomer (2003) likens this quick text identification to turning on the TV, glancing at the show, and—even if he's never seen it before—being able to figure out what kind of show it is because it "fits" into something he *has* seen before. Even though I've never watched a "cop" show, I can pick one out with just a quick glance . . . and then turn the channel. The cop shows look quite different from the sitcoms or documentaries for which I'm searching. As a reader, when you picked up this book from the shelf, you quickly realized, just by looking at the cover, that it was a professional text—a text from one educator to another. Therefore, you are most likely thinking that you will learn some new information that you can add to your current understanding and philosophy about supporting readers in your classroom. You have certain expectations about how this text will "go." When I pick up a memo from my mailbox at work, I know that there will be important information presented in short, terse writing. I'm expecting that the information on the memo most likely concerns something that impacts my fifth graders—the social studies test, middle school applications, or graduation. Whether it's a professional text or a quick memo, knowing the genre of the text and having expectations of it allows us to *more skillfully* read the text itself. It's as if we put a frame around our thinking *before* we start reading, helping us to contain our thoughts to both a specific purpose and a certain genre. When we engage in this essential prereading skill, we set ourselves up for a more successful comprehension of the text.

Although most of my experience is with third, fourth, and fifth graders, I have had opportunities to work with younger students. Coaching kindergartners to engage in prereading behaviors is not that different from coaching ten-year-olds. I'll say to Adam, a five-year-old with a Level D book in his hands, "Watch me as I look at the cover of this book. I see a jungle gym, some swings, and some kids playing. I'm thinking that this book will be about playgrounds. I'm thinking that I'll read about the different things that can be on a playground. Let's take a book walk and see what we find." Before Adam delves into his book, I show him how to preview the text and have expectations. He knows that his book will be mostly about playgrounds. As he narrows his focus for reading, he will be more successful in understanding the short story about playgrounds. In my fifth-grade classroom, I make a similar teaching point with Arlinda, who holds a Level S book in her hands. Before Arlinda turns to the first page in her novel, she employs a fundamental reading skill—

Feb. 8

Previewing for Growing Plants

1. It's non-fiction
2. looks like a ▓▓▓ artical
3. there are pictures
4. captions/labels
5. difficult words
6. it's detailed
7. how to guide (piece)
8. set up
9. life cycle (beginning)
10. timeline
11. instructions

(11)

previewing the text and having expectations—which helps her frame her purpose for reading and generating ideas about the text.

Previewing novels is one thing, and previewing shorter texts is another. I use the teaching structure of both minilessons and weekly shared reading to reinforce the transfer of prereading skills from genre to genre. When a text structure looks unfamiliar and daunting, my fifth graders seem to abandon what they know about smart prereading behaviors, like previewing the text and having expectations. Exposing my students to many different types of genres and text structures helps ease their apprehension and enables them to approach any text with a strong prereading plan. Applying this prereading skill ensures that readers will more successfully comprehend the text itself.

## Doing a Double Take: Locating Oneself in the Text

Once proficient readers have previewed the text, identified the genre, and thought about their expectations for the text, they locate themselves in the text by utilizing some key reading strategies: activating prior knowledge, making connections, having questions, and determining importance. Locating oneself in the text strengthens one's active engagement with the text, improving fluency and expression while reading and encouraging appropriate reaction to the text. A fluent, expressive reader who reacts and responds to a text demonstrates his strong comprehension of the text.

### Activating Prior Knowledge

A key reading strategy, activating prior knowledge is essential both before reading and while reading. Once proficient readers set their purpose for reading, based on their preview of the text, they think about what they already know about the text topic. Activating prior knowledge helps readers ground themselves in their current understanding of the topic before they read to both confirm their thinking and learn new or conflicting information about the topic. Readers continue to activate prior knowledge while they read as they revise their thinking and ideas. Most often, my fifth graders activate prior knowledge when they read nonfiction texts; a text titled *It's a Mammal!* (Stewart 2004) naturally inspires my students to think about what they already know about mammals. Once they have secured themselves in their current knowledge about mammals, they are ready to read and learn more about mammals. However, proficient readers activate prior knowledge when they read any genre, not just nonfiction. My fifth-grade readers are quick to forget to recall what they already know about a topic if the text genre is a poem, a map, or even a story. Again, I use both minilessons and weekly shared reading to help students practice this reading strategy on a variety of text genres. In order for students to locate themselves in the text successfully, they must first consider their existing knowledge.

### Making Connections

As proficient readers read, the information from the text reminds them of stories or ideas from their own lives, other texts they've read,

What is the genre?:

| poem |

How do you know?

- The lines are broken
- Each sentence is a capitol
- ★ It can't be a non-fiction piece because there are no facts!
- ★ It can't be fiction because there is no fantasy!

or ideas that exist in the world. These connections are deeper than "Oh, the character in this book has a cat, and so do I," as they spark readers to react and respond to the text. As I read *A Million Little Pieces* (Frey 2003), I began to understand the same harrowing cycle of despair and desolation that also exists in *Random Family* (LeBlanc 2003), and I was moved to learn more about drug addiction and abuse and align more of my volunteer efforts with supporting recovering addicts. Not every connection readers make will be as reactionary and life changing as this one, but the effect of all powerful connections is the same—they enable the reader to more deeply understand the heart of the text. When readers understand the heart of

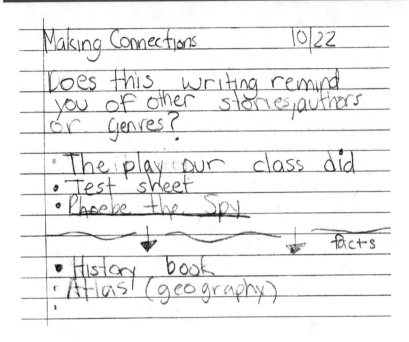

the text, they further engage as active participants with the text. A quick scan of the classroom during independent reading allows me to see which readers are reacting to the text and which readers are not; facial expressions, gasps, giggles, and tears demonstrate a reader who is making connections from the text to the world beyond the page. While my fifth-grade readers are more successful in making connections to realistic fiction stories, other text genres can prove to be just as engaging and thought provoking. Demonstrating reacting and making connections to poetry and nonfiction structures, and allowing time for my students to practice this strategy on these text genres, encourage them to make connections that deepen understanding when they read a variety of texts.

## Having Questions

Proficient readers have questions beyond simple plot predictions (e.g., Will Ramona get in trouble for cracking the egg on her head?) that

Open-ended ✓          9/28
        Other Side

• Why did Clover's mom
say not to stare to
Clover?

• Did this happen to
Jacqueline Woodson?

• Clover's mom was
happy when she found
out that Clover made
a friend (Annie)

• Is this story true?

• Since Clover is Annie's
friend, Sandra probaly
said "I dont care." because
she wants to be friends
too.

encourage them to seek answers both inside and outside the text. Having questions is another reading strategy that enables readers to locate themselves in the text. By asking questions, proficient readers are engaged in reading, are committed to the text, and interact with the text to construct meaning. As fluent readers search for answers within the text and outside the text—through discussion or written response—they monitor their comprehension of the text. As I model this strategy for my students, I strive to make it clear that skilled readers question the text as a way to interact and make meaning of the text, *not* just to have questions that go unanswered or are answered on the following page. I remember cringing as I watched third grader Christian write questions on sticky notes and slap them on every page of his book, never once stopping to consider, answer, or reflect on the sea of yellow stickies that were expanding his novel like an accordion. Just as I stress to my students that when they make a connection while they are reading, they need to stop and think about how that connection helps them to understand the text, I remind them that when they have questions while they are reading, they need to stop and think about how those questions help them understand the text.

## Determining Importance

Proficient readers set a frame for their reading and thinking when they preview the text and have expectations. In essence, they determine a focus and a purpose for their reading before they delve into the text. For example, they may read to remember and confirm information, or they may read to learn new information and build their content and background knowledge. When skillful readers set a purpose for their reading, they also determine what's important in the text. Readers can locate themselves in the text by determining and thinking about the important ideas in the text. When I read aloud to my students, I model how I have hunches about what are the big and important ideas in the text. I explore my hunches as I read, noting substantiating evidence. I distinguish the important information from the interesting information, showing students that proficient readers are quite discerning. Determining important ideas and information in the text allows readers to make meaning of the more sophisticated upper-grade texts.

## Filling in the Picture: Envisioning

During a Calendar Day at Teachers College, Randy Bomer (2003) presented his thinking concerning readers; the presentation, titled "Minds on Fire: Teaching Readers to Think as They Read," detailed the kinds of thinking that are useful in reading comprehension development. When he came to envisioning as an essential reading skill, Randy bluntly stated, "The text is describing a picture to you as a reader. If you don't see the picture, you're not understanding the text."

Proficient readers envision while reading to *fill in the picture* in order to ensure their comprehension. Envisioning goes beyond "making a movie in your mind" and encompasses the picturing of ideas and abstract concepts. A fluent reader sees the text in his mind's eye, regardless of the topic, genre, or text structure.

Stories lend themselves to envisioning so naturally that it is easy for me to show students how I create a movie of the text in my head, whether I'm reading *or* writing a story. Stories offer an imaginable context in which the plot develops, in which characters interact, and in which a problem arises and is (potentially) solved. Fluent readers can see, in their mind's eye, the characters and the action of a story. Although the details of the characters' faces may differ from reader to reader, the images are clear and enhance the meaning of the text. One of my favorite read-aloud books for fourth graders is *Holes*, by Louis Sachar (1998), because it so encourages readers to envision the story. The images of desolate Camp Green Lake, the unique and charming characters in the story, and the intricately woven plot haunt my nine-year-olds for weeks after I finish the book. Of course, a book this rich in imagery was made into a popular movie. I couldn't resist traipsing with thirty-six fourth graders around New York City so we could see one of our favorite stories on the big screen. In the dark theatre, throughout the entire movie, my students expressed their shock and annoyance because they didn't picture the characters, setting, or action in the way the movie portrayed them! As a fluent reader, I could relate, as I recalled how the movie versions of books often fall short of the movies that I created in my own mind's eye. The power of envisioning is that it both heightens engagement with the text and deepens comprehension.

Envisioning goes beyond creating a movie of the text in one's head—proficient readers also envision ideas and abstract concepts. Transferring this powerful reading skill from one comfortable genre—story—to other genres is essential and important, yet uncomfortable and unfamiliar for my upper-grade readers. Think about reading about an invisible idea, like evaporation, or an abstract concept, like government. Proficient readers can visualize diagrams (the water cycle) and spatial metaphors ("sections" of the U.S. government) in their mind's eye. Some nonfiction texts offer visual supports, like charts, maps, and pictures, to scaffold the work for readers. However, nonfiction readers still must fill in the picture and

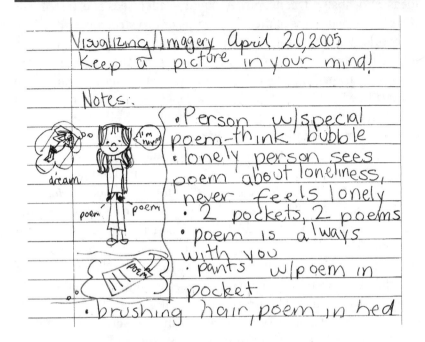

see all pieces and ideas of the text together to fully understand it. Poetry typically offers no pictorial support, challenging the reader to create images from a text with a more flexible and unpredictable structure. During weekly shared reading, students can practice the skill of envisioning on these more challenging types of text, strengthening the transference of the skill from genre to genre. By noticing and visualizing content words, comparisons, and figurative language, students are enabled to approach a variety of texts and apply the skill of envisioning, which will in turn augment their comprehension of the text.

## Digging Deeper: Inferring

Inferring—reading the world around us and reading between the lines of a text—is one of the most important and sophisticated life skills *and* reading skills to teach and learn in upper-grade classrooms. In life, reading people's body language, tone of voice, and eye contact will make our interaction with them much more appropriate and produc-

April 14, 2005

**Perspective**

- Author's purpose/message

C — the whole poem is
        important
    - nothing to throw
      away
    - all parts important
    to meaning
    - you keep a poem

T — dig in, get involved
Me
    - poem is good, like
    good food
    - so good, can't stop
    "eating," can't throw
    away
    - always good
    - enjoy the poem
    - different kinds
are juicy

tive. As communicators, we infer that furrowed eyebrows and pursed lips probably mean that our boss is in a sour mood, and that we should stay away until further notice! How do we know that? We look at the clues—furrowed eyebrows and tight lips—and think about what we already know about those gestures. Putting the clues and our background information together, we make a smart inference.

In reading, proficient readers use key information from the text and their prior knowledge to infer ideas and theories about the text. The implication is, then, that readers are able to identify the important information in the text and also possess a breadth and depth of background knowledge about life and the world. Skillful readers do not utilize reading skills in isolation, but in conjunction; the ability to infer is built from the abilities to have expectations of the text, locate oneself in the text, and envision. During weekly shared reading, I can provide more practice for my students to determine important information in the text while, through exposure to various texts, they build their background knowledge in efforts to strengthen their inferring skills.

Readers who infer understand both the tone of the text and the big ideas in the text that also exist in the world. Authors' perspectives are woven throughout the more sophisticated texts in upper-grade classrooms. Most often, authors write with an angle, subtly expressing their feelings about a topic or an idea. Additionally, humor and sarcasm make their way into the texts that are enjoyed by our older readers. Readers who can infer authors' perspectives and the tone of the text will naturally be more engaged with the text, thereby possessing a more solid understanding of the text. When I see students reading the ubiquitous Series of Unfortunate Events, by Lemony Snicket (1999–2006), I expect to see them smirking, shaking their heads, or even laughing out loud. Proficient readers who infer the ripe sarcasm and not so subtle thoughts about societal values will enjoy and understand the series much greater than readers who remain on the literal level.

Inferring big ideas in the text that exist in the world also solidifies readers' comprehension of the text. The most meaningful ideas from the text often stem from what readers infer, not from what's written on the page. When I read *Hoot*, by Carl Hiassen (2002), to my fourth graders, I very clearly shared my thinking about the bigger ideas in the story, derived from the details in the text and my own background knowledge. Soon, my students were just as passionate about animal rights as the characters in the book. The power of inferring, as evidenced by social action on the part of my students, allows readers to further capture and understand the heart of the text.

I notice that my students find identifying authors' perspectives and recognizing bigger ideas beyond the text more challenging in some texts and in some genres than others. I encourage students to

**Author's Purpose**

→ To show facts

→ What life is like in the 1700's

→ Give ex. of what people said & did

→ To tell history in a fun way

→ Give historical info. about Sons of Liberty

→ To make this time in history imp

→ Gives ex. from past that is similar to the present

→ Love of history

see the author's angle and understand the bigger idea from a nonfiction piece during both minilessons and weekly shared reading. Again, supporting my readers in utilizing the skill of inferring across all texts strengthens their inferring muscles and allows them to understand a deeper meaning of the text.

## Getting the Big Picture: Synthesizing

As proficient readers read, they continually fold their ideas together to create the greatest understanding possible. They use their

Figure 2-8    After spending a week with the text, Tringa records potential conversations she could have about Cynthia Rylant's "Spaghetti" (1985)—or any text, for that matter. Throughout the school year, students like Tringa realize that general themes that exist in the world also exist in different texts. Tringa has moved beyond the literal and narrow confines of the text and is thinking more globally, about themes and bigger ideas in a text.

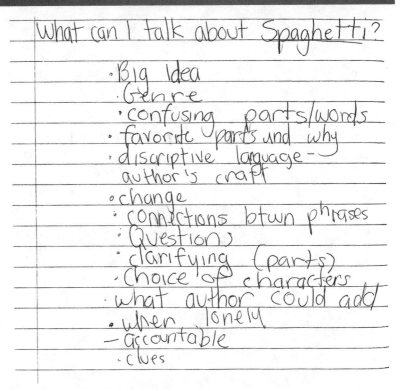

What can I talk about Spaghetti?
- Big Idea
- Genre
- confusing parts/words
- favorite parts and why
- discriptive language — author's craft
- change
- connections btwn phrases
- (Question)
- clarifying (parts)
- Choice of characters
- what author could add
- when lonely
- accountable
- clues

knowledge and their reading to synthesize the information and ideas at hand. When proficient readers finish a text, they can tell you, in a few words, what the text was mostly about *and* the ideas they have about the text. This reading skill is quite complex, as synthesizing information demands that readers *constantly* revise their thinking as they read. When readers synthesize information, they can put down a text and feel like they own it, meaning that they are able to have an informed and deep conversation about the whole text.

When readers aren't synthesizing, it's written all over their faces. Their engagement in the text wanes, and their reaction to the text falters. Sliding up to a distracted child for a reading conference, I

*Text Savvy*

quickly know that Molly isn't synthesizing the information and ideas from her chapter book because she shares small and trivial details from the story when I probe her for the ideas she's having while she's reading. In a nonfiction text about sharks, an unengaged Mohammed can point to each part of the busy page, sharing facts he's learning while he reads, but he can't tell me what the page is mostly about and what his thinking about the text is. These two students, like many others, are not getting the big picture—they aren't synthesizing while reading and aren't able to engage in accountable talk about the text.

Readers who synthesize monitor their comprehension as they read. They use strategies like rereading, stopping and thinking, jotting notes or underlining text, reading in manageable chunks, and talking to a partner. Through minilessons, I model these fix-it strategies to ensure synthesis and comprehension, but in weekly shared reading, I have students synthesize information and ideas with me, using fix-it strategies as we go. I have come across some readers during my time in the classroom who thought that they weren't supposed to understand what they were reading. Because they didn't understand the text, they didn't know that their comprehension had broken down, and so they didn't know *how* to monitor for meaning and use fix-it strategies. Having my upper-grade readers, especially these struggling readers, work through a text with me, and synthesize information with me, supports them in developing their independence as more fluent readers.

Talk—in a large group, in a small group, or between partners—is one way for readers to express their ideas and thoughts about a text and strengthen their understanding of a text. When readers synthesize as they read, their talk will be about ideas, wonderings, and theories about the heart of the text. On the other hand, imagine Molly engaging in partnership talk, sharing her small details from the text with her partner, or Mohammed sharing facts from his text. Readers can talk about ideas from a text, but they really can't talk about details or facts from a text. Yes, Oliver will perform in the school talent show, and sharks do have a lot of teeth, but what is there to talk about and discuss? It would be quite different if Molly and Mohammed had *ideas* about the details and facts in their texts. As Molly read, if she synthesized the details from *Oliver Button Is a Sissy* (dePaola 1979) and her ideas from the story and said, "Oliver is really brave," she would open up a conversation with her partner. If

What We Could Talk About...
- style of the writing (flashback, diary)
- confusing words and parts
- connection / comparison to other texts
- a shocking part / unexpected
- questions / thoughts
- why was Sons of liberty a secret
- reminds you of...
- time period
- genre
- story elements

Mohammed synthesized the information and ideas from the text about sharks and said, "Sharks have a lot of teeth to help them survive the dangerous waters," his partner could respond as well. Solid, accountable talk is grounded in synthesis and ideas that readers have while they read.

# Ongoing Reflection

In my classroom, I strive to continuously deepen my students' reading and thinking work. As I think about Tringa's progress as a reader, I feel that through weekly shared reading, I was able to explicitly show her *how* to proficiently read a variety of texts. Through the rereading of texts and focused practice, she was able to demonstrate the reading skills and strategies that proficient readers utilize when they tackle a variety of text genres and structures. Tringa was pushed to think deeply about texts; she was encouraged to move beyond the literal interpretations of the texts and to move toward big ideas. She was also supported as she tackled new vocabulary in more sophisticated texts. As Tringa encountered increasingly complicated texts, it was critical that she understood how the five essential reading skills were used not in isolation, but interdependently. Weekly shared reading provided the ideal vehicle, allowing me to model the strategies and skills of a proficient reader.

Tringa might remind you of students in your classroom—proficient yet literal, slowly building vocabulary—a solid 3 as measured by the state reading assessment. Weekly shared reading can help push readers like Tringa from a literal reading life to a grander reading life—from a 3 to a 4, from meeting the standard to exceeding it. The interpretive work, scaffolded by class discussion, allows students like Tringa to challenge themselves and open doors in reading that they never knew existed.

# Big Ideas from Chapter 2

- Proficient readers integrate five essential reading skills as they read to ensure comprehension of any text.
- Through weekly shared reading, along with other instructional opportunities, reading comprehension strategies that build these five skills are modeled and practiced.

# *Weekly Shared Reading*

# 3

## *A Day-by-Day Account*

# Monday: Having a First Glance

On a wintry New York City morning, my colleague Wendy Binkowitz gathers her third-grade students to the meeting area. The overhead is prepared with the weekly shared reading text for the week. This week, Wendy has chosen a short nonfiction text about spiders. Wendy has noticed that her students are reading bits and pieces of a nonfiction text, but are not synthesizing their prior knowledge and the new information they are learning. She has also noticed that some nonfiction texts are completely overwhelming to her kids— their eyes move quickly over the page, looking at chunks of text, captions, headings, and diagrams, unsure of where to start reading. Even though she explicitly teaches nonfiction reading strategies during her minilessons, she knows that her students need additional practice to build the five essential reading skills.

"OK, readers," begins Wendy. "We know that every time readers look at a new text, they ask themselves, 'What genre is this text, and what are my expectations for the text?' Let's do that together with this new text on the overhead."

Wendy flicks on the overhead to reveal a one-page nonfiction article about spiders' lifestyle, spiders' bodies, and some differences between spiders and insects.

"Hmm . . . I'm thinking that this is a nonfiction text, because I see photographs of the topic, spiders, and some other nonfiction features. What are you thinking? Turn and talk with your partners."

At this point, Wendy listens in on partnership conversations between Adel and Barbara, and Jessie and Colette. Quickly, Wendy brings her class back to attention.

"Readers, Jessie and Colette pointed out that the headings and subheadings clued them in that this was a nonfiction piece as well. Adel and Barbara noticed the bold words in the text, and they thought those were content vocabulary words, which we see in many nonfiction texts. So, as readers, we're identifying this as a nonfiction text.

"Previewing the text helped us get familiar with how this text is set up. I have a better plan in my mind for where I'm going to start reading—right here, the text under the biggest heading." Wendy points to a spot in the text that is a natural starting point. "We've previewed the text; now let's think about our expectations for the text."

Hands shoot up across the rug, as students are eager to share their expectations.

"Jason? What are you expecting from this text?"

"I'm thinking that I'll probably learn something new about spiders when I read this because I don't know a lot about spiders."

"William?"

"I'm expecting that the text has facts about spiders, like facts about their bodies and life and stuff."

"How about you, Pauline?"

"I know a lot about spiders, so I'm thinking that I might know everything already in the text!"

"Turn and talk to your partner—what are your expectations for the text?"

At this point, the room erupts with conversation. Wendy scoots to the back of the rug and listens in on a few partnerships.

Wendy moves back to the overhead, saying, "So, we all have expectations about the text. Some of our expectations are the same, like we know there will be facts about spiders, and we might learn something new. Some of our expectations are different, like Pauline mentioned that she might not learn anything new. So let's put a frame around our reading. We're reading to confirm our thinking about spiders, like Pauline, and we're reading to learn something new about them, like Jason. Listen and follow along with your eyes as I read the text out loud."

Wendy reads the short nonfiction text, modeling the behaviors of a fluent and expressive reader. She reads slowly, using a different voice than if she had been reading aloud a story.

"Readers, what did you already know, and what information was new? Turn and tell your partners."

Again, Wendy listens in on the conversation. Each time she listens in, she's assessing on the run, thinking about what her students are saying and thinking.

To keep within a short time frame, Wendy closes her weekly shared reading lesson, saying, "So, some of our thinking was confirmed, and some of our thinking changed! Tomorrow we'll be working on locating ourselves in this text by having questions about it."

### READING SKILL: PREVIEWING THE TEXT AND HAVING EXPECTATIONS

| Possible Question or Noticing to Elicit Skill | What It Might Sound Like in a Real Classroom |
|---|---|
| "Here's what I'm noticing about this text that makes me think it's nonfiction . . . What are you noticing?" | "Adel and Barbara noticed the bold words in the text, and they thought those were content vocabulary words, which we see in many nonfiction texts." |

# Tuesday: Doing a Double Take

Wendy's kids move swiftly from their tables to the meeting area for the second day of weekly shared reading with the spider text. From yesterday's quick assessment, Wendy can confidently say that her students were able to proficiently identify the text's genre (nonfiction) and set up expectations for a reading of the text. Today's focus is on building the reading skill of locating oneself in the text, and Wendy has chosen to highlight the strategy of questioning.

"Readers, yesterday we previewed the text and had expectations for it. We knew it was a nonfiction text by the text features, and we expected that we would know some information in the text and learn some new information. Today we are going to locate ourselves in the text by having questions before, during, and even after we read. Now, the thing about having questions before and while readers read is that the questions can't just go unanswered. The questions we want to ask are the questions that will help us to better understand the meaning of the text.

"So . . . before I read this text on spiders, I'm wondering, 'Can spiders be helpful to us?' What are your questions about the topic before we read? Turn and talk."

Students' chatter fills the room and Wendy listens in to assess the kinds of questions students are asking.

"Hmm . . . I'm hearing Ursula ask, 'Are all spiders poisonous?' and Jeremy wonder, 'Can spiders kill you?' I'm thinking that the three of us have a similar wondering about spiders—how dangerous are spiders? Let's read with that question in mind."

Wendy reads the text out loud as students follow along with their eyes. Again, she uses a slow yet fluent and expressive voice. Wendy stops after she reads that spiders eat pesky insects that destroy crops.

"Wait a minute . . . it sounds to me that spiders are helpful to farmers because they eat pesky insects that destroy crops. How does that help us begin to answer our question? Turn and talk."

Students acknowledge that maybe not all spiders are dangerous, and they can even be helpful at times. Wendy restates, "So, we're learning about a time when spiders are helpful and not dangerous. Our question is really helping us understand the text better. But this is only one example. So let's keep reading."

When Wendy finishes the short piece, she reflects on the question the class pondered before reading. "Our question, 'How dangerous are spiders?' helped us to understand the text better because we realized that spiders can be helpful too. Is anyone still curious about this question? Turn and talk."

Wendy's students still want to know how dangerous spiders are—could they kill us? Wendy acknowledge her students' questioning minds.

"Readers, you are so smart to have questions after you've read a text! Sometimes the answers to our questions are not discovered while we read, so that means we have to do more thinking and maybe more reading to find an answer with which we're satisfied."

Zachary pipes up, "I bet you could look in other books about spiders and figure out how dangerous they are!"

Wendy agrees. "Right—the beauty of nonfiction reading is that you can read about a topic across books. So we could look in some other spider books for the answer to our question."

Wendy ends her session by saying, "So, readers, today's questioning helped us begin to understand the meaning of the text in a deeper way. Tomorrow we're going to visualize to further deepen our understanding."

| READING SKILL : LOCATING ONESELF IN THE TEXT | |
| --- | --- |
| Possible Question or Noticing to Elicit Skill | What It Might Sound Like in a Real Classroom |
| "These questions help me understand the text because . . ." | Wendy restates, "So, we're learning about a time when spiders are helpful and not dangerous. Our question is really helping us understand the text better." |

# Wednesday: Filling in the Picture

Kids are clamoring around the overhead as Wendy sets up for weekly shared reading.

"Wendy! Wendy! Not all spiders are dangerous, but some are, like the black widow spider!"

Wendy mentions, "That's such a responsible thing that readers do—if they have questions once they finish reading, they make the effort to find the answers themselves!"

Wendy quickly reflects that her transparent modeling of asking and answering questions during yesterday's weekly shared reading

*Text Savvy*

session supported her students in constructing content knowledge about spiders, but it may not have helped them become any more adept in using the strategy of asking questions before, during, and after reading. She makes a mental note that she'll need to highlight the strategy of asking questions in next week's weekly shared reading lesson.

Wendy presses on. "So today, readers, we are going to further make meaning of this text by visualizing—making a picture in our minds. Let's look at this first chunk of text." Wendy directs her students to look at the first of two chunks of text. This chunk describes the body of a spider.

"So, I'm going to start reading and really picture what's going on in the text in my mind. I'm not going to read this really quickly, but I'm going to read it slowly and I'm going to stop and examine the picture in my mind."

Wendy begins reading, noting that the bold words are the vocabulary words that describe the spider's body parts. "So . . . the abdomen is the large rounded end of the spider. I'm going to picture that in my mind—you do it with me. What do you see?"

Kids with their eyes closed shout out, "Big and black!" "Rounded." "Fat." "Shiny and round." "Biggest part of the spider."

Wendy listens to her students' comments and then shares one with the group: "Gertrude was describing a black jelly bean for the abdomen, which is a smart idea. Readers can always compare an unfamiliar picture, like a spider's abdomen, to a familiar one, like a jelly bean.

"Let's picture the head now. What do you see?"

This time, students use similes and metaphors in comparing the head to more familiar objects. Wendy takes note and shares the images with the class.

"So, readers, how has the picture of a spider changed in your mind, from what it was to what it is now that you've really pictured it?"

Yolanda says, "I wasn't picturing the two parts of the spider, but now I am."

Brandon says, "I can see each part of the spider in more detail."

Winston adds, "I used to just picture the eight legs of a spider, but now I can see the whole thing!"

Wendy sums up, "So readers, when you slow down and visualize, the picture in your mind can be so powerful. It will help you understand the text much more deeply. Tomorrow we'll practice inferring the big idea from the text."

| READING SKILL : ENVISIONING | |
|---|---|
| Possible Question or Noticing to Elicit Skill | What It Might Sound Like in a Real Classroom |
| "What do you see in your mind's eye?" | "So . . . the abdomen is the large rounded end of the spider. I'm going to picture that in my mind—you do it with me. What do you see?" |

# Thursday: Digging Deeper

Wendy's students once again are seated around the overhead, looking at the shared text on spiders. Wendy feels that her readers were successful in envisioning the spider's body parts yesterday, and that envisioning work has prepared her students to do the harder work of inferring today. Wendy plans to assist her readers in making inferences about the big ideas in the text.

"Readers, the past few days we've been unpacking this text. We oriented ourselves to the text and confirmed our expectations about it. We asked ourselves questions before, during, and even after we read the text, in order to deepen our understanding. Yesterday, we envisioned as we read, really thinking about the content vocabulary words in the article and picturing the spider's body parts in our mind's eye. We've learned many facts about spiders from this article, but today we're going to work on making inferences—thinking about the big ideas that exist beyond the text.

"So, when I read this part, 'Some spiders are helpful to farmers because they eat pesky insects that destroy crops,' I began thinking that some animals that we think are dangerous and scary might actually be helpful, and we just don't know it. I'm thinking that this is a big idea that the author is trying to get across—animals are not always dangerous, but can be helpful too.

"I'm going to reread the article today; this will be our fourth reading of it. We know it pretty well by now. As I read, I want you to be thinking of the text's bigger ideas—what big ideas does the author want us to learn?"

Wendy knows that her students experience difficulty with inferring and typically resort to making literal predictions about possible events in the text. Weekly, she presents another opportunity for her students to practice inferring in a very supported environment.

Wendy finishes reading the piece. "Turn and talk to your partner. What are some of the text's bigger ideas?"

Wendy grabs her anecdotal record-keeping sheet and listens to five or six partnership conversations. She's quickly assessing on the run, determining if students are successfully inferring. She chooses to share the clearest inference from one partnership, Gabriel and Michael.

"Readers, from the line 'Spiders and insects are not to be confused,' Gabriel and Michael inferred that spiders and insects must be so different for many reasons. Gabriel and Michael, would you like to add on?" Wendy gently prompts the partners to share their thinking with the group.

Michael says, "We thought that the author wants everyone to know that spiders and insects are really different, and that's an important thing to know and remember. Maybe the author gets upset when people call spiders insects and insects spiders."

| READING SKILL: INFERRING | |
| --- | --- |
| **Possible Question or Noticing to Elicit Skill** | **What It Might Sound Like in a Real Classroom** |
| "I wonder why the author wrote this article?" | "We thought that the author wants everyone to know that spiders and insects are really different, and that's an important thing to know and remember. Maybe the author gets upset when people call spiders insects and insects spiders." |

Wendy validates Michael's thinking. "What a smart inference! You are really thinking about the big ideas from the text and what the author wants us to learn.

"Tomorrow, readers, we'll synthesize this text, putting everything together from the past week, in preparation for our conversation."

# Friday: Getting the Big Picture

Wendy reflects on her students' practice during this weekly shared reading cycle. Her assessments tell her that her students are becoming very secure in previewing the text and having expectations and envisioning, but they are still not as independent in questioning and inferring. Wendy makes note of their progress and will use this information in planning for future instruction in all balanced literacy structures.

Through her support, Wendy's readers will be able to synthesize the text during weekly shared reading today, although she realizes that without her support, her students might not get the big picture.

As her students gather on the carpet, Wendy holds onto these thoughts and proceeds with the fifth and final day of this week's weekly shared reading text.

"When good readers read, they are constantly stopping and thinking, 'How has my thinking changed, based on what I've read?' This helps them synthesize the text, or put it all together. We're going to reread the text, stopping and thinking, 'How has our thinking changed?' as we prepare for a conversation about this text."

Wendy begins reading the nonfiction article. She stops a few sentences into the text. "So, this part here, 'Some spiders are helpful to farmers because they eat pesky insects that destroy crops,' changed my thinking. I didn't know that spiders were helpful. Stopping and realizing this has helped me to understand the text.

"I'm going to keep reading, and I'll stop after every chunk—after every paragraph. You'll turn and talk to your partners: Did your thinking change? What do you think now?"

Wendy continues reading the text, stopping six more times and allowing students to talk to each other about their changes in thinking. By allowing her students to engage in partnership talk, Wendy prepares them for a whole-class conversation about the text.

"So, now that we've finished reading and synthesizing the text, we're ready for our accountable conversation about the text." Wendy's students make sure that they are in a circle so that everyone can be seen and heard. The text remains on the overhead so that students can refer to it during the conversation.

"Who would like to start the conversation?" Wendy prompts. "You can think about starting with how your thinking changed as you read this text."

For the next five minutes, Wendy's students are engaged in a back-and-forth conversation about the changes in their thinking. Most students were surprised by information about spiders and revised their thinking about this topic. Throughout the conversation, Wendy listens closely, looking for her students to support their thinking with evidence from the text.

At the end of the weekly shared reading session, Wendy distributes copies of this week's text to her students. They each place their copy in their weekly shared reading folders and can refer to it as needed.

| READING SKILL : SYNTHESIZING | |
|---|---|
| **Possible Question or Noticing to Elicit Skill** | **What It Might Sound Like in a Real Classroom** |
| "How has my thinking changed?" "How have I revised my thinking?" | "So, this part here, 'Some spiders are helpful to farmers because they eat pesky insects that destroy crops,' changed my thinking. I didn't know that spiders were helpful. Stopping and realizing this has helped me to understand the text." |

# Ongoing Reflection

Oftentimes at home, and certainly in preschool and kindergarten, students listen to and learn storybook language through the rereading of favorite picture books and fairy tales. Young students come to understand narrative texts; they understand how a story goes. Therefore, it's not surprising that most students become very fluent and proficient in reading this particular genre. They are able to use what they know about story to have expectations of the text, to make connections to the characters, to visualize the action in their minds, to think beyond the tale, and to talk about the narrative. As these children move into the upper-elementary grades, though, they are confronted with texts in a variety of more *unfamiliar* genres. As teachers, we can build on what students do well with story by modeling for them how to read different genres. This modeling can take place through many instructional opportunities—the read-aloud, the minilesson, the teaching point in a conference, and weekly shared reading.

Wendy's selection of a nonfiction text is smart in that it exposes her third graders to an increasingly common text genre and structure that exists in the upper grades and beyond, it provides an opportunity for Wendy to model the habits and skills of a successful and fluent reader of nonfiction text, and it gives Wendy a window into her students' tenuous understanding of the marriage between the five essential reading skills and the genre of nonfiction.

# Big Ideas from Chapter 3

- While the five essential reading skills remain the same from week to week, the reading strategies modeled and practiced vary from week to week.
- Weekly shared reading can introduce readers to less familiar text genres and structures in a supportive setting.
- A teacher's reflection on her students' learning informs future weekly shared reading instruction.

# Assessment

4

### Eliana

Eliana, a fifth grader, would always go above and beyond what was expected of her. She was the type of student who got it from the get-go. She shared insightful ideas during our whole-class conversations. She moved beyond literal interpretations and thought very deeply about her reading. The question was: How should I support her? How could I push her thinking even further?

# The Power and Possibilities of Assessment During Weekly Shared Reading

When students are faced with new, challenging genres, assessment becomes key. As their teacher, it is critical that I stay on top of my students' current reading levels (remembering that it might vary from genre to genre) and place books in their hands that they can truly read. Weekly shared reading provides me with a much-needed safety net; it gives me an additional opportunity to assess their understanding of the varying, complicated genres my students encounter. *It allows for a more public demonstration of their reading strategies, thereby enabling me to more thoughtfully support them as they move toward independence.*

The possibilities for assessment during weekly shared reading are manifold:

- The teacher can extend the "with" phase: he can watch students work through the text as they talk about it with a partner and the whole class, and assess their current level of understanding.
- Weekly shared reading enables the teacher to assess on the run, noting a great number of students' strengths and needs in a communal setting.
- Weekly shared reading helps the teacher evaluate the "stickiness" of teaching from unit to unit. For instance, while nonfiction reading strategies might be taught in depth in November, it is important to assess whether the students still understand and utilize these reading strategies throughout the school year. Weekly shared reading allows the teacher to continually reassess what the students have retained from previous units of study.
- The teacher can use assessments to lift the level of students' future reading work.

## Slowing Down the Gradual Release of Responsibility—Extending the "With"

Come into my room on any given day and you'll see me explicitly modeling during a minilesson, listening to my students as they turn and talk to their partners after a think-aloud, conferring with individual students, and celebrating their newfound ownership of skills and strategies during independent reading. The balanced literacy model empowers my students—they're encouraged to delve deeply into each unit of study, to take on the powerful work of readers.

The *gradual release of responsibility* inherent in this model reminds me of learning how to ride a bike. I didn't just get up one day and ride a bike around my neighborhood; it was a process that took time, energy, and support. Similarly, my upper-grade students won't fluidly move from familiar fictional texts to content-rich nonfiction texts and complicated historical fiction novels on their own; they need scaffolded supports as they transition into this heady work.

Sometimes, though, I feel that the transition from holding on to my kids' metaphorical handlebars to letting go is too quick. I want to linger longer with my upper-grade readers as they navigate these new texts—I want to extend the "with" phase. In addition, because I can get to only a couple of kids a day, I worry that some of my students might (unbeknownst to me) tumble, that I won't be there to pick them right back up, that I won't be there at the moment when they need me most. I'm catching them days later, wondering why I didn't earlier recognize their difficulty with reading a time line or their confusion with how a historical period impacts the characters' actions.

With weekly shared reading, I'm able to work through a text with the students—the training wheels get to stay on a bit longer. As opposed to a think-aloud, which is where the teacher models reading skills and makes them visible, or independent practice, weekly shared reading is a bridge between the two, where readers have more time to practice with a fluent reader, developing sharper reading skills. There is additional time for practicing reading strategies together on a variety of texts across genres. It extends the "try it with me" phase of a minilesson, small-group work, conference, or guided reading session, thereby ensuring that the release of responsibility is indeed gradual.

## Working Through a Text During Weekly Shared Reading

On Monday, when the students in room 5-306 first looked at the text "An Immigration Nation" (Satterfield 2006), we focused on the genre and the setup. Arlinda was able to easily identify it as a nonfiction text; on a sticky note, she quickly wrote, "Nonfiction: It has titles, subtitles and graphs." As I walked around the classroom, I noted that everyone in the class had identified the genre correctly. On Tuesday, as I listened to Arlinda's conversation with her partner, Victoria, I was happy to hear them co-identify the big idea: "This text is mostly about immigration and what the president is doing to support immigrants." I was excited to know that they could clearly narrow down the article to a few concise lines.

Because of the time constraints placed on me as a teacher, I often *stop* at the metaphorical Tuesday, when my students have comfortably located themselves within a text, when they know the genre and can summarize. I might decide that since they've met my expectations—Great! They know how to identify the elements of the nonfiction genre; they're able to clearly summarize what the text is mostly about—I must move on to other students who are still struggling with those important, foundational pieces. But what about the Elianas in my classroom—those students who are soaring, moving above and beyond the literal interpretations? I need to ensure that those students' needs are also being met. The weekly shared reading model allows my class to linger, to develop a much deeper understanding of the genre and relevant reading strategies.

As the week went on, our weekly shared reading conversations were deeper, more reflective. Together, the students and I cocreated knowledge. On Thursday, Derek noted that the article really addresses only the president's point of view; he pointed out that there were no quotes from actual immigrants, there was no understanding of their perspective. By Friday, after talking to his talk partner, Reese shared with the whole class that he hadn't thought about the fact that immigration was going on *now*. "I thought it happened one hundred years ago, at Ellis Island." By returning to this text over the course of the week, I was able to realize that while I might have taught my students how to identify the main idea of an article, I hadn't taught them how to truly incorporate their new knowledge into their larger worldview. On their own, they weren't thinking about how this text changed their thinking, their ideas about immigration. They were looking at this piece in isolation, not seeing *how it changed them*. Only by returning to it again and again was I able to truly understand what I still needed to teach and were they truly able to do this work.

Weekly shared reading provided me with another opportunity to assess my students, to watch them work through a text. By slowing down the release of responsibility—extending the time in the "try it with me" phase—I was given another opportunity to listen to their conversations, ask for in-the-moment responses on sticky notes, and engage in extended discussions. I got another glimpse into their understanding of the chosen genre and which reading strategies they were most likely to rely on when reading this genre. By going back to the text again and again, I found that we were able to get into the nuances, that I was able to identify what I needed to revisit when planning and teaching. After our week with the nonfiction article "Immigration," I realized many things: I needed to make a more explicit effort to highlight the connections between immigrants from the past and the present during our social studies unit on immigration; in my future nonfiction instruction (and maybe in my instruction of all genres), I needed to push my students to think about how the nonfiction reading changed them as readers and as people. I started thinking about how I hadn't really emphasized that skill—maybe because I'd taught that unit in November or maybe because I hadn't associated that skill with nonfiction reading. By having this extended time with this one text, outside of the current unit of study and with my students, I was able to assess what they understood and reassess what I still needed to teach.

When extending the "with," my students' training wheels were on, and my arms were securely holding onto their handlebars. I guided the students through the process, helped them understand *what it felt like* to truly grasp this particular genre. While they might not have been able to do this work without me, they were on their way to taking ownership. I know that if we'd only spent a few minutes referring to this piece as a nonfiction mentor text, they would have learned how to identify the genre, how to find the big idea. I'm not so sure, though, that this deep analysis would have happened. Not only did my students reevaluate their world perspective, but also I reconsidered and deepened my understanding of my own instruction.

Ultimately, one of the greatest outcomes of extending the "with" phase is that, as a result of looking back at the same text over the course of a week, the classroom takes ownership of *this* text, *these* skills, and *these* strategies. Weekly shared reading texts aren't the typical mentor texts that a teacher might stay with, at most, a couple of times or that a student might take on as his own individual mentor text. The weekly shared reading texts and the work done during those fifteen-minute increments become shared knowledge—everyone in the class owns the text and the ideas that grew during the weeklong discussion. During the "with" phase, I guide them; help them understand what it feels like to envision, to infer, to synthesize. I give them the opportunity to work through a strategy, to try it on for size. I might introduce something that is out of their independent reach, but that they can take on with the support of their classmates and me. By continually revisiting previously introduced genres, the teacher provides the students with the opportunity to take more ownership of their learning and enables the students to move toward the "by" phase, toward independence.

## Shared Reading

### Three Branches of Government

Previewing:

→ Punctuation is used to help me navigate the text as a reader.

→ Three branches must be imp. b/c of way the page is set-up

→ Bold lettering — what you should notice first/pay attention ti

→ "New" genre — nonfiction Diagram

Accountable Talk Ideas:

- What the author wanted to show/teach you
- Set-up - Is it interesting to you as a reader?
- Why these Branches are imp. / What they do?
- The 3 main branches of Gov. are very important.

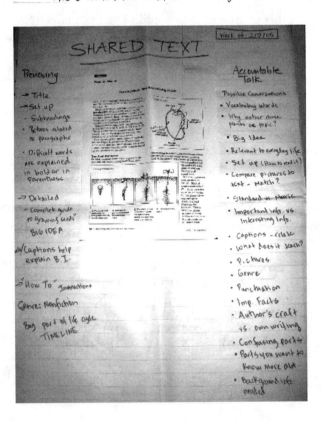

**WORKING THROUGH THE TEXT:**
**ONGOING OPPORTUNITIES FOR ASSESSMENT**

- use of stickies, notebooks
- listening to conversations between talk partners
- cocreated  conversations
- cocreated  charts
- considering how skills and strategies filter into other subject-area work

## Assessing on the Run

We all do our very best to get to know our students well; we meet with them during writing conferences, we listen to their conversations during their turn-and-talks, we reflect on their published pieces. Still, it often feels as if there is never enough time. So, in an effort to address our concerns, Christine Lagatta, one of our staff developers from the Teachers College Reading and Writing Project, introduced us to assessing on the run.

Assessing on the run literally adds time to my day—it is a structure that allows me to note a greater number of students' strengths and needs within a communal setting. As opposed to getting into in-depth discussions with a handful of kids, I am able to reach *more* kids over a *shorter* period of time. After showing them a strategy, I move from partnership to partnership rapidly, watching them try it, assessing their understanding. It helps me see the big picture—I am able to quickly develop an overall assessment of my class as a whole and the kids' grasp of genres, skills, and/or strategies. It affords me another, swift opportunity to check in with more of my students.

While one-on-one conferences are still necessary and important, the reality is that as upper-grade readers get into these new, more challenging texts, it's essential that I quickly assess what they understand, catch them *as soon as* they begin to fall, and rescue them *before* they get too lost. Assessing on the run during weekly shared reading helps me further evaluate their understanding of the concepts and strategies taught during reading and writing workshops.

The flexibility of this structure means that what my assessment during weekly shared reading might look like or what my focus might be can change *within the moment*. For example, if, on a given Wednesday, I ask my students to sketch a picture detailing a moment of tension in the story, but I find that they're all drawing a picture detailing an irrelevant event, then I can quickly change the course of my weekly shared reading. I might decide that in order to better grasp the skill of envisioning, they could switch strategies—instead of sketching, they could talk to their partners so they could construct the image *together*.

So, if I want to go beyond the metaphorical Tuesday—and I must; I owe it to my students—I should introduce or reinforce the strategies that help build and solidify the more sophisticated reading skills. The excerpts in Figures 4–2 through 4–7 demonstrate how Eliana was challenged to think deeply about texts while remaining accountable. In Figure 4–2, Eliana lists all of her noticings—the title, the bold words, the author, the paragraphs. Beyond that, though, she starts to make inferences; she finishes off the entry by noting that it's a nonfiction piece of writing. She shows that, given what she knows about different genres, all of these features come together like pieces of a puzzle to make a nonfiction piece of writing. In Figure 4–3 (page 52), she draws a picture, but beyond that she takes the time to identify the key words—the essentials—in the text. Even though it's early in the week, she holds onto all of the strategies that were introduced to her throughout the year. She is able to synthesize the text into a few words. In Figure 4–4 (page 53), Eliana lists words in the text that are unfamiliar to her. She knows she should understand the whole text, and when she doesn't understand something, she notes it. Furthermore, she thinks about what she would need to do to understand those words. In Figure 4–5 (page 54), Eliana shows that beyond having ideas about a text, it's important to support her thinking with facts. She uses evidence from the text to ground her opinion. It's interesting to note that she identifies a couple of ideas about the text—she realizes that there isn't one pat answer, that there is room for different ideas or interpretations. In Figures 4–6 and 4–7 (pages 55–56, Eliana dives deeply into the text and then beyond it. She synthesizes *everything*—she asks questions, notes big ideas, identifies a metaphor. She has internalized the text; it has changed her thinking about the world. *This is the work of a reader*—Eliana could easily take these notes to a book club meeting or use them to write a thoughtful literary essay.

> # Previewing the Text
>
> ## How the Text is set up
>
> - There's a title: it's in bold letters
> - There are lines seperating different parts of the text
> - There are big, bold words in the middle of the text
> - It's a newspaper article
> - There's an author, and information about the author
> - There are paragraphs
> - It's non-fiction

*Possible Strategies to Be Introduced/Reinforced
During Weekly Shared Reading*

- bulleting (see Figure 4–2)
- sketching images (see Figure 4–3, page 52)
- highlighting vocabulary words (see Figure 4–4, page 53)
- synthesizing and inferring (see Figure 4–5, page 54)
- preparing for talk (see Figure 4–6, page 55)

Assessing on the run informs my future minilessons, conferences, small-group work, *and* weekly shared reading instruction. My
findings can help me decide what needs to be revisited. If I find that
during that day's lesson, my students didn't entirely grasp how to access prior knowledge by asking themselves, "What do I already know
about this topic?" then I can return to that very same strategy during
weekly shared reading.

The reality is that the stakes for upper-grade readers are high. My
students *require* a strong reading foundation—they need to have

flexibility within and among genres. The amount of individualized instruction that I'm able to provide them is limited; still I need to deeply scaffold their understanding before sending them off. Assessing on the run during weekly shared reading allows me to reach more kids over a short period of time. As an upper-grade elementary teacher, it is critical that I know where my students are, so I can move them toward where they need to go.

All readers in my classroom have access to the weekly shared reading texts, and I support their engagement and understanding through my modeling, questioning, and probing. Highly skilled readers, like Eliana, are pushed to grow their complete understanding of texts through conversation, writing, and sketching. Weekly shared reading ensures that the Elianas in my classroom are challenged yet supported.

> Parts of the Text
> Where you need Backround
> Information
>
> • abuelito, Esta muereto — you
> Would have to Speak Spanish
> to Know those words

## The Stickiness of Our Teaching

Each month or every six weeks, my students and I deeply delve into a genre we get to know narrative or fiction or poetry *really well*. We share the language—we speak it, read it, and write it every day. Considering this, it's not surprising that everyone is going to be familiar with it, demonstrating some level of fluency. What happens, though, when students leave that unit of study? What happens when we're not in a poetry unit of study, but the students are asked to engage with and respond to a poetry text? How can I assess the "stickiness" of my teaching?

While I truly appreciate the focused depth that the balanced literacy model affords me as a teacher and my students as readers, I believe that it is important for my students to continually exercise *all* of their reading muscles. One of the constraints of the balanced literacy model is that it is designed in such a way that most of my instruction and assessments—during active involvement, small-group strategy lessons, and one-on-one conferences—relate to our *current* unit of study. In reality, though, as a reader I might read the newspaper in the morning, a memo at work, a novel on the subway, and so on. Considering this, my students should be provided with instruction in and ongoing assessment of *a variety of genres*. Weekly shared reading alleviates this concern, by varying between text genres week to week. It provides my students with the opportunity to

## Identifying Perspective

### Artist's Purpose

I think this artist is trying to show how horribly people are treated, and how unfair things can be, also I think the artist is trying to show that noone should be treated differently than anyone else. Also, you should be grateful for what you have.

### Evidence:

- they're tied up
- they have no food and no clothes
- there is a man with a spear guarding them

flex their various reading muscles and enables me to monitor my students' ongoing growth in *all* genres.

Another of the constraints of balanced literacy is that over the course of the year, we do not have the chance to spend a lot of additional time instructing our students in certain genres. We may spend only six weeks teaching nonfiction. While our study is in depth, our explicit instruction of this genre takes place once a year. While we know we are building upon the work done by the teachers before us, we often feel like we're reteaching concepts. If a student is asked to

Figure 4–6   After spending a week with the text, Eliana records her thoughts and potential conversations about *Fly Away Home* (Bunting 1991). The type of conversations she chooses go beyond the confines of the book.

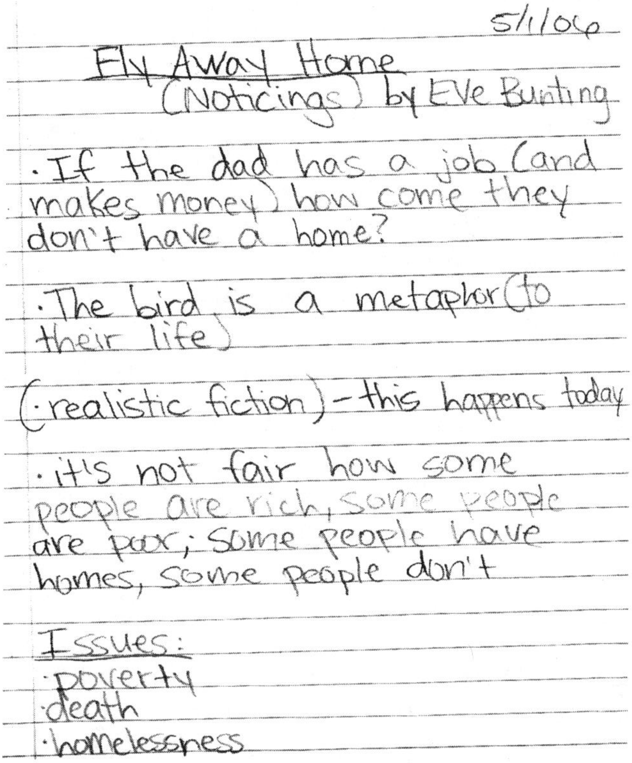

5/1/06

Fly Away Home
(Noticings) by Eve Bunting

· If the dad has a job (and makes money) how come they don't have a home?

· The bird is a metaphor (to their life)

(· realistic fiction) — this happens today

· it's not fair how some people are rich, some people are poor; some people have homes, some people don't

Issues:
· poverty
· death
· homelessness

think deeply about poetry only during the month of April, it's no wonder that the following year she exhibits a vague, superficial knowledge for her teacher. Furthermore, a teacher doesn't get the benefit of knowing that the students have held onto knowledge that was taught months earlier. Not only are the students limited in their opportunity to work those genre-specific muscles, but teachers are limited in their ability to evaluate the endurance of their teaching over the course of and throughout the years.

The consistency of the weekly shared reading structure allows for flexibility within our units of study. We can comfort ourselves with the knowledge that we won't and *shouldn't* get to everything, that we can continually return to different genres over the course of the year.

Figure 4–7

```
                                            5/2/06
        Fly Away Home

    BIG IDEAS:

    · It's not easy to be homeless
    · Don't give up
    · Anything is possible
    · there's always hope
    · Even though life is hard, you
    have to try to hang on
    · Being homeless impacts your
    life
    · there's always something in
    life that's not fair
```

Realistically, we know that we can't and shouldn't get to everything within one unit of study. We need to pick and choose. During our realistic fiction unit of study, we may decide to focus in on envisioning and synthesizing. We know that it is best that our students do a couple of things very well, as opposed to wading in whole lot of mediocrity. When we leave a unit, though, we might find that there are certain skills or strategies that still need attention. We celebrate the strategies the kids took on as their own, but questions still exist: What if we could have lingered with the author's perspective? Why didn't we think to spend more time preparing for accountable talk? The weekly shared reading model allows us to dip back into the units— maybe we realize that we need to revisit and strengthen their understanding of certain strategies and that *now* is the time to reinforce this skill.

My principal, Adele Schroeter, asked our community to think about the "stickiness" of our teaching. If we taught historical fiction in

*Text Savvy*

February, would our students retain what we taught later on that year? The following year? How were we, as educators, checking in with our students? How were ascertaining whether they had internalized our explicit instruction? Taken it on as their own? Thinking back to that moment during weekly shared reading when everyone in my class was able to identify the genre as nonfiction while we were reading "Immigration" was exciting for me. As it was now May and nonfiction hadn't been explicitly taught since last November, I was able to assess that my direct instruction months ago had *stuck*—my students had internalized the features of this genre. If our ultimate goal as educators is to guide our students toward independence, we need to find as many ways as we can to support them on this journey.

Figures 4–8a through 4–8c (see pages 58–60) show an essay Eliana wrote, building upon the work we did during weekly shared reading. Through assignments like this, I am able to assess what the students have held onto from the whole-class discussions and my teaching. Furthermore, I am able to encourage students to think deeper, to push themselves further.

## Continually Lifting the Level of Their Work

Weekly shared reading affords me another opportunity to check in with my students, to ascertain their understanding of current, past, and future units. With this deeper assessment, I am able to lift the level of their work, both during weekly shared reading and within the traditional balanced literacy structures. Because of its cyclical structure, weekly shared reading can be viewed as a time to strengthen weaknesses found during other subject areas or to illuminate the focus of my future instruction. The work done daily during this fifteen-minute period allows the class to venture into past and future units of study. Not only does this reinforce lessons previously taught, but also it introduces students to upcoming concepts and genres.

## Using Assessment to Inform Future Instruction

Let's return to Wendy's third-grade classroom to see how she used assessment as a means to prepare her students for the upcoming standardized test. While they had spent a lot of time getting ready for the test, she found that her students were still struggling with the various features of nonfiction. Even though they had deeply

Essay                                    1/23/06

Have you ever done something to make the world a better place? Well, there are lots of ways you can! The characters in Martin Luther King's speech, A Day's Work, Riding the Tiger*, and The Other Side did. You can make the world a better place by standing up for what you believe in, helping someone out, and doing what you think is right. You can make the world a better place!

You can make the world a better place by standing up for what you believe in. In Martin Luther King's speech, Martin Luther King stood up for the rights of black people. In The Other Side, Clover and

immersed themselves within the genre months before, she realized that they were still new to this work and that the time set aside for nonfiction instruction hadn't been enough. Her students needed to do more work within that genre. As a result, she decided to reformat her weekly shared reading for her students.

Instead of following the prescribed method—four different genres over the course of a month—she chose to plan for one fiction piece, one poetry piece, and *two* nonfiction pieces every month. By providing the students with additional opportunities to see different types of nonfiction, she was better able to assess whether it was the particular genre or certain features that were really tripping her students up.

Figure 4–8b

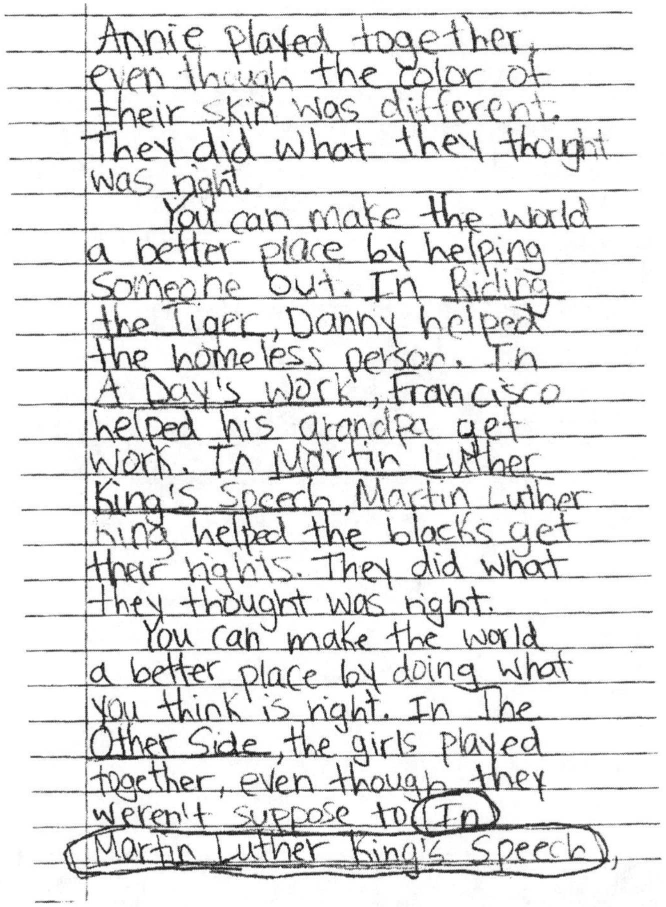

Annie played together, even though the color of their skin was different. They did what they thought was right.

You can make the world a better place by helping someone out. In Riding the Tiger, Danny helped the homeless person. In A Day's Work, Francisco helped his grandpa get work. In Martin Luther King's Speech, Martin Luther King helped the blacks get their rights. They did what they thought was right.

You can make the world a better place by doing what you think is right. In The Other Side, the girls played together, even though they weren't suppose to In Martin Luther King's Speech,

Likewise, when she found that a particular strategy was sticking, but other strategies were not, she planned accordingly. Under the umbrella of envisioning, she might ask her students one day to create a movie in their mind, but another day challenge them to use a graphic organizer. Ultimately, her goal was strengthening their understanding of this complicated genre, moving them toward mastery of each strategy within each skill. Since she knew that it was not possible to do all the necessary teaching and learning during the designated reading and writing times, she spent more time on it during weekly shared reading. In order to best meet her students' needs, she continually assessed their understanding and continually reevaluated her planning.

Figure 4–8c

Martin Luther King [6] stood up for black people's rights. In Riding the Tiger, Danny got off the Tiger's back. They did what they thought was right.

Don't be afraid to do what you think is right! You can do something to make the world a better place, even if it's something as little as holding the door for someone else. If characters in books can make the world a better place, than so can you.

Table 4   Ways to Lift the Level of Students' Work During and as a Result of Weekly Shared Reading.

| Teacher | • asking guiding questions<br>• reevaluating own instruction<br>• introducing challenging concepts in a supportive environment |
| --- | --- |
| Partner | • contributing to the whole-class discussions<br>• asking questions<br>• challenging presented ideas |
| Self | • self-monitoring due to the metacognitive nature of this cyclical model |

# Assessment Opportunities During Shared Reading: A Month in a Third-Grade Classroom

Table 5   Week One: Nonfiction Article

| Strategies | Assessment Opportunities |
|---|---|
| • previewing text<br>• scanning page and pointing out features<br>• defining genre<br>• confirming genre after text is read<br>• setting expectations for the text | • listen in on partnership conversations; use anecdotal recording sheet/assessment checklist<br>• students jot their thinking and evidence on sticky notes; collect and review<br>• students mark up their own copies of the shared text; review and assess |
| • thinking, "What do I know about this topic already?"<br>• thinking, "What might be new information for me?" | |
| • reading and thinking, "What is this mostly about?"<br>• chunking the text; paraphrasing after each chunk<br>• determining important versus interesting information (higher-level thinking—incorporate as year progresses) | |
| • using context clues to solve for unknown words<br>• using text features (e.g., bold words, glossary on bottom of page) to solve for unknown words | |
| • reading and thinking, "What do I know *now* about this topic? Where is the evidence to support my thinking?"<br>• reading and thinking, "What questions do I still have? "How could I answer those questions?" | |

## Table 6    Week Two: Poem

| Strategies | Assessment Opportunities |
|---|---|
| • previewing text<br>• scanning page and pointing out features<br>• defining genre<br>• confirming genre after text is read<br>• setting expectations for the text | • listen in on partnership conversations; use anecdotal recording sheet/assessment checklist<br>• students jot their thinking and evidence on sticky notes; collect and review<br>• students mark up their own copies of the shared text; review and assess<br>• view sketches/images of the feelings and thoughts the poem evokes |
| • thinking, "What do I know about this topic already?"<br>• thinking, "What do I know about this poet?  Have I read any of her other poems?"<br>• thinking, "What do I know about poetry?  How will it help me read this poem?" | |
| • reading and thinking, "What is this mostly about?"<br>• chunking the text in stanzas<br>• inferring: thinking beyond the text using clues from the poem<br>• sketching the images and feelings that come to mind when reading the poem | |
| • using context clues to solve for unknown words<br>• using features of the poem (e.g., rhyme) to solve for unknown words | |
| • reading and thinking, "What is the author's message?  What is the evidence to support this?"<br>• reading and thinking, "What will I keep thinking about after I say good-bye to this poem?" | |

Table 7    Week Three: Excerpt from Current Read-Aloud

| Strategies | Assessment Opportunities |
|---|---|
| • previewing text<br>• scanning page and noting features (e.g., characters, dialogue)<br>• defining genre<br>• confirming genre after text is read<br>• setting expectations for the text | • listen in on partnership conversations; use anecdotal recording sheet/assessment checklist<br>• students jot their thinking and evidence on sticky notes; collect and review<br>• students mark up their own copies of the shared text; review and assess<br>• students set up their thinking in a T-chart (theory about character/evidence to support theory); students can continue this chart during the read-aloud time and use a similar template for their independent reading |
| • thinking, "What do I know about this story already?"<br>• thinking, "What do I know about this author? Have I read any other stories from him?" | |
| • reading and thinking, "What is this mostly about?"<br>• chunking the text; using dialogue, breaks in a chapter, change in setting, and so on to stop and paraphrase story's events<br>• determining who's talking (if dialogue is unassigned)<br>• attributing voice and phrasing to the text<br>• visualizing: creating a movie in the mind | |
| • using context clues to solve for unknown words<br>• substituting other words that would make sense for unknown words<br>• substituting a pronounceable name when a name is unknown or difficult | |
| • rereading for humor and deeper meaning<br>• making generalizations, generating theories about characters, using evidence to support thinking<br>• having ideas about the story events | |

Table 8   Week Four: Map of the United States*

| Strategies | Assessment Opportunities |
|---|---|
| • previewing text<br>• scanning page and noting features (e.g., key, shading, scale)<br>• defining genre<br>• orienting self to the text (reading a map)<br>• confirming after text is read<br>• setting expectations for the text | • listen in on partnership conversations; use anecdotal recording sheet/assessment checklist<br>• students jot their thinking and evidence on sticky notes; collect and review<br>• students mark up their own copies of the shared text; review and assess |
| • thinking, "What do I know about this topic already?"<br>• thinking, "What might be new information for me?" | |
| • reading and thinking, "What is this mostly about?"<br>• chunking the important parts of a map; stopping after each chunk and paraphrasing information | |
| • using context clues to solve for unknown words<br>• using a more familiar context (e.g., own experiences with maps) to solve unknown words or ideas | |
| • reading parts of map and thinking, "What do I know *now* about this topic? Where is the evidence to support my thinking?"<br>• reading and thinking, "What questions do I still have? How could I answer those questions?" | |

* In third grade, teachers found it necessary and beneficial to have two nonfiction pieces per month.

# Ongoing Reflection

As is the case with the rest of my balanced literacy work, I need to remind myself that weekly shared reading is *not* a script—it demands interplay between the teacher, the students, and the structure. Ongoing planning, instruction, and (most importantly) reflection are required. If all texts were planned out at the beginning of the year, then there would be no point to using this structure. Weekly shared reading is designed to support the fluid, ongoing, and important work started and revisited during the rest of your balanced literacy periods.

The beauty of this structure is that it is designed to support *all of my students*; the collective conversation grows everyone's knowledge. For a student like Eliana, who does not always demand immediate attention because her skills are so solid, this structure is perfect. It is designed to deepen her thinking and understanding; I am able to lift the level of her work, value her voice, and encourage her to reach new heights.

I encourage you to revisit your plans, to reevaluate a chosen strategy. As educators, it is necessary that we continually assess our students' work and our own teaching. I believe that weekly shared reading completes the balanced literacy circle of instruction.

# Big Ideas from Chapter 4

- Weekly shared reading extends the "with" phase during the gradual release of responsibility.
- Assessing on the run during weekly shared reading provides another opportunity to identify students' immediate needs.
- Assessment gathered during weekly shared reading informs future instruction in other balanced literacy structures.
- Weekly shared reading offers teachers the opportunity to evaluate the stickiness of their teaching.

# Supporting Struggling Readers

# 5

# Amber, Molly, and Bernard

Amber, a third grader, was paradoxically determined and disinterested in her schoolwork. She eagerly participated in every class discussion, her hand waving frantically in the air, but often "forgot what [she] was going to say" when it was her turn to contribute. She wanted to please her teacher by being ontask during independent work time, but instead, she routinely socialized. She wanted to lead the book club discussion, but she struggled to comprehend the meaning of the text. Amber wanted to be a fluent reader, but she needed a boost to overcome her obstacles.

Molly, with her pigtails and freckles, appeared to be a quintessential third grader. Her sweet smile and quiet way in the classroom made her most endearing. On the playground, however, Molly teased other kids, pulled pranks on her classmates, and tested authority. Her teacher attributed her dual personalities to her intense struggle in school, especially in reading.

Bernard was a quiet and somewhat sullen fifth grader. He tried to keep his struggle with reading from his new teacher, but she quickly realized his despair. He had given up on growing as a reader; he would choose texts that were way too difficult for him, read for only a few minutes, and then begin to distract his classmates or daydream. His indifference as a learner was both worrisome and heartbreaking.

Our instructional plans consider the engagement and access of our most struggling readers. These are the kids who are on our minds when we go to bed at night. Will they be able to do the work?

Will it make sense to them? And how will they progress as readers in a timely, yet supportive fashion?

In every classroom, a reality exists—the reality of a range of readers. From struggling and in desperate need of intervention, to excelling and in obvious need of challenge, the readers in our classrooms demand our most creative, planned efforts in instruction in order to meet their needs and assist them in achieving their reading goals.

The structures of balanced literacy offer multiple opportunities for such focused instruction; the work time in the reading workshop lends itself to purposeful small-group instruction, targeted to meet the specific needs of groups of students. Concurrently, weekly shared reading provides additional support for our range of readers, from the most tenuous to the most advanced.

Readers like Tringa—proficient yet literal—are in our classrooms. Readers like Eliana—advanced and eager—exist as well. The snapshots from their classrooms provide a sense of how I was able to push their thinking and support them as budding readers through weekly shared reading. But what about our struggling readers—the Ambers, the Mollys, the Bernards? How can weekly shared reading support them?

# The Sophisticated Nature of Upper-Grade Texts

As my upper-grade students move beyond a reading world filled with fiction stories, archetypal characters, and familiar plots, they chart unknown territories. When my students' decoding ability starts to outpace their full and complete understanding of the more sophisticated texts found in upper-grade classrooms, there is a comprehension breakdown. Say, for example, in a Level P reading bin, one of my students finds both *A Taste of Blackberries* (Buchanan Smith 1973), a narrative fiction text that parallels an ordinary child's concerns and experiences, and *Time Warp Trio* (Scieska 1991), an adventure book that requires the reader to possess historical background knowledge and an understanding of sarcasm in writing. There is a big difference between these two books—different reading strategies are needed, as are different levels of background knowledge. A student without the proper historical briefing and sense of sarcasm is not going to fully get *Time Warp Trio.*

Beyond the range of text choices available on one level, there is also the reality of content-rich reading in the upper-elementary grades. Never before have my students been bombarded with dense science texts, informative social studies documents, and increasingly complex nonfiction pieces. As I introduce a historical fiction unit of study, expose them to primary source documents, and watch them reach for dense nonfiction scientific magazines, questions arise: Am I providing the scaffolds that can ensure they will successfully take on these new reading challenges? Am I certain that they are reading these various genres with true comprehension? Are they strong enough readers to know when they are lost in these complicated texts?

# Am I Meeting *All* of My Students' Reading Needs?

When students read, their reading and thinking work is invisible. I have many structures in place to help me get a glimpse of what students' minds are doing when they read. When I slide up to a student for a one-on-one conference, I can assess a student's fluency, word-attack strategies, and comprehension. I encourage students to use sticky notes or keep a reading notebook to jot their thinking as they read. I listen in on partnership conversations, learning about the reading strategies students are using as they read and talk about books. These structures help me make my students' reading work more visible, but I can assess only a few students over the course of a day. While I have a strong handle on what those particular readers are doing, it might take me two weeks to have individualized conferences with everyone. I worry about the students I haven't yet met with, the readers that might be struggling through complicated texts.

In the back of my mind, I'm not 100 percent convinced that every kid is reading with comprehension; the fluctuation in text demands and the constraints of our units of study make me wonder how to best support all of my readers on their way to independence.

## Casting Off the Invisibility Factor

I know my students as readers—I learn about their strengths and struggles during read-aloud, in small groups, and in individual conferences. But I really learn about them during weekly shared reading; working through a text hand in hand casts off the invisibility factor of their reading and thinking work, and I am privy to their insights and misconceptions. Weekly shared reading offers opportunities for me to assess my students' understanding of reading and thinking skills—*and* the stickiness of my teaching. I can quickly tweak a weekly shared reading session as I move through it, based on my students' more immediate needs, but when I sit down to plan my literacy instruction, I am sure to reflect on the conversations and my notes from those efficient and focused ten to fifteen minutes a day. My constant reflection during and after a weekly shared reading session shapes my future instruction in balanced literacy.

## Moving Forward

The very nature of shared reading supports struggling readers, just as it supports emergent and early readers in primary classrooms. The teacher reads the text, modeling the skills of reading with fluency, expression, and phrasing—the building blocks to reading with meaning and comprehension. Struggling readers in the upper grades still need to see *how* to read with fluency, expression, and phrasing. The weekly shared reading texts are short, highly interesting, and manageable; the class rereads the text and returns to them throughout the week; the classroom community makes a collective meaning of the text together. These components of weekly shared reading also support struggling readers as they build their repertoire of habits that successful readers use while working through a text.

Weekly shared reading offers all students various entry points into the conversation around a text. As a class, we make meaning of the text together, in a supportive environment. I guide and steer the conversations under the umbrella of the five essential reading skills, but I don't hold the only keys to understanding the text. Weekly shared reading empowers students, encouraging them to take on the challenging yet rewarding work of readers.

Following are vignettes from my school of some struggling readers. Weekly shared reading allows teachers to have a window into their students' understanding and offers ideas for future instruction.

# Amber: Seeing Herself as a Reader

Amber pulls the books from her book bin as she prepares for reading workshop. She splays them out on the table in front of her. Her third-grade teacher, Jennifer Chalfin, quickly glances at her books to make sure they are appropriate for this budding reader. She notices two Level L books—perfect for Amber—and one much more challenging Level P text. Amber waffles between reading an L or the P, running her hands over both texts. Jennifer watches with some concern, wondering why Amber chose a book that she knows is too challenging for her. Abruptly, Amber stands up with the P book in hand and skips over to the classroom library. She places the P book back in its bin and returns to her seat, picking up one of the L texts and opening it. Jennifer quickly walks over to her.

"Amber, I noticed that you had a Level P book in your book bin, and you decided to return it to the library. Why did you do that?"

Amber looks at Jennifer with a serious and dramatic expression on her face. "Wellll, I *really* want to read that book, 'cause Reem said it's *really* good . . . but it's too hard for me right now. This one here is better for me as a reader."

Knowing herself as a reader is new to Amber. Amber's teacher feels that weekly shared reading has transformed students like Amber, and offers the following reflection:

> Weekly shared reading helped build confidence for all learners (especially struggling learners), and allowed them to have familiarity with texts across days. It also allowed to me quickly assess through listening in on conversations as well as times the kids stopped and jotted. Overall, weekly shared reading

was extremely effective and insightful. It allowed me to teach so many different skills and strategies and embedded all the genres that kids read. Kids applied the work we did to all structures of reading (independent reading, partnership reading, book clubs, and test taking).

Amber is on her way to becoming a proficient reader, and she has already overcome some hurdles that may hold other struggling readers from moving forward and making progress. Foremost, Amber *sees herself as a reader*, one who demonstrates good reading habits of choosing and reading books independently, and thinking and learning while reading. She knows that print holds meaning, so she is committed to reading the texts that allow her to be successful at meaning making. Because she knows that reading is supposed to make sense, she also knows that there are books in the world that she cannot read and understand at this time in her reading life. However, Amber knows that *she will become a more skillful reader over time*, and soon she will be able to read the more challenging texts—like the Level P book—with understanding.

Weekly shared reading can be the bridge between the read-aloud and independent reading that students like Amber desperately need in order to push themselves into *being accountable to a text*—something that they cannot quite yet do on their own.

# Molly: A Nonreader Pushed into the World of Reading

Molly positioned herself on the floor for independent reading. As the rest of the third-grade class settled into the silence of engaged readers, Molly struggled like a restless sleeper—tossing and turning on the carpet, trying to find a comfortable position. Eventually, she opened her book and began thumbing through the pages. She glanced around the room. She took the ponytail holder out of her hair and twirled her long locks in her fingers. She flipped onto her back, then her side. The book closed. With one hand in her hair and the other in the book, she awkwardly attempted to find a good starting point. She began turning the pages, one by one, and continued to look around the room.

At this point, I looked at the clock. Independent work began at 10:15 A.M. It was now 10:30 A.M. Wendy Binkowitz's most struggling reader had spent fifteen minutes of precious reading time completely unengaged in her book. Wendy and I know that the best thing for struggling readers is to have their eyes on print in order to truly improve their reading skills, but how were we going to convince Molly that she needed to spend her independent work time *reading and thinking*?

Wendy and I consulted each other before we approached Molly, brainstorming why she was so unengaged. Was the book too difficult for her as a reader? Was she perhaps not interested in the genre or subject matter? Was her reading spot not the best choice for her?

Molly watched Wendy and me walk over to her; she immediately chose a random page and pretended to read. As we sat down next to her, she peeked at us from the corner of her eyes.

"Hi, Molly," I started. "You know, I was watching you from across the room, and I noticed that it took you a while to get started on your reading work. It seemed like you couldn't get comfortable, that you weren't sure where you left off in your reading yesterday, and that you were distracted by people and other things going on in the room."

At this point, I just stopped and looked at Molly. She sheepishly smiled and nodded her head.

"Can you talk to us about what's going on?" I probed.

Molly shrugged.

"Well, Molly, when I see kids who aren't engaged in their books—and instead are looking around the room, moving their bodies around, thumbing through their books—I get a little confused. I'm wondering, 'Why isn't Molly reading? Maybe the book is not right for her as a reader right now. Maybe she doesn't like the genre or subject matter. Maybe her reading spot is not so great.' So, let's figure out, together, what's going on with your reading life. Can I listen to you read for a while?"

Molly glanced down at the book.

"Why don't we start at the beginning?" I suggested.

*Text Savvy*

Molly turned to the first page and began to read out loud. Her expression, fluency, and phrasing suggested that the text level was appropriate for her—appropriate for applying reading skills in order to understand the story.

Wendy flipped through her anecdotal records. "Molly, I notice you're reading a Nate the Great mystery [Sharmat 1972–2006] . . . and you've read these books before during this school year. Do you still like them?"

"Yeah," Molly said. "In every book, Nate has a mystery to solve, and he figures it out."

Wendy and I glanced at each other. The text itself was manageable and Molly had the general gist of the series, but it didn't seem like she was really *thinking* and *working* while she read.

I pressed on. "What about your reading spot? Is this the best choice for you?"

Molly slowly shook her head from side to side.

"So, what do you want to do about that?"

She shrugged.

"Want to move up to a chair and table? It might help you feel less distracted."

Molly left the carpet and picked a spot at a table with one other reader.

"So, Molly," I began, "it seems like this is a just-right book for you because you are 'reading like you're talking,' and you like the series. We've changed your reading spot. Now I'm wondering, 'What's the work you're doing while you read?'"

She looked at me blankly.

"Well, like when I read, I'm thinking about my expectations for the text—I'm thinking about what I already might know about the topic, I make connections from the text to my own life, I picture what's going on in my mind, I try to figure out what the author really wants me to take away after I'm done . . . do you do any of these things?"

"I make predictions," Molly stated.

"What predictions are you making with this text?" I asked.

"I predict that Nate will solve a mystery," she said.

My conversation with Molly confirmed my thinking that she was indeed a nonreader—she was decoding the words, but she was not engaged in the text, and therefore not fully, or even partially, making meaning of the story. Molly had mastered the art of being unaccountable to a text; her vague synopsis of the story and obvious prediction suggested that she didn't necessarily need to read that text to come to those conclusions.

Molly couldn't afford to remain unengaged during independent reading. Instead of planning a barrage of intensive one-on-one conferring sessions with Molly, Wendy and I turned our efforts to weekly shared reading. We felt that Molly needed *more time to practice*, alongside us, the five essential reading skills and the myriad strategies that proficient readers use to activate these skills. Molly needed to experience *what it feels like* to be a proficient reader. She wouldn't necessarily have this experience during independent reading, but she was much more likely to have it during weekly shared reading.

Wendy and I looked at Wendy's weekly shared reading plans. Wendy wanted to revisit a realistic fiction narrative throughout the week. As we selected an engaging text and then tweaked the strategies that Wendy would teach, ensuring that they were transparent and accessible, we thought about Molly's needs. The first form of shared reading children experience is when infants sit on their caretaker's lap, listening to a story over and over again. We concentrated on how to get Molly "in our lap"—to be right there with us as we read and thought about the text. We felt our text selection was engaging and relevant, and it was on a lower reading level than we would have otherwise selected. We planned our turn-and-talks with focused questions and prompts. And during the talking and discussion, we would be listening to and coaching into Molly's conversations.

As the week unfolded, Molly stayed "in our lap." We guided her, with a heavier hand, through thinking about the text in the way that proficient readers would. We whispered in her ear, prompting her to say smart things during conversations. We followed up with her after weekly shared reading and suggested she sketch the picture in her mind's eye of the story she was getting to know so well. At the end of the week, during our class conversation about the text, Molly was able to refer back to the text itself, pulling evidence to support a classmate's idea. After the conversation, we pulled her aside and told her *that's* what it feels like to be an accountable reader! *That's* what it feels like to know a text, to think about it, and to understand it. And

Molly's crooked smile confirmed our efforts in helping her experience the world of reading.

Wendy reflected,

> Shared reading does not alienate any student. It does not discriminate reading levels or achievement. Everyone participates and everyone goes off with a new strategy or way of looking at text each day . . . all on the journey leading to greater independence when tackling various genres in reading.

After our concerted effort with Molly during weekly shared reading, Wendy and I monitored her closely during her independent reading time, looking for signs of engagement, and conferring with her to check for her understanding of the text. We noticed that she was more proficient in reading and understanding books in the same series, so we encouraged her to remain in a series for a while before moving onto another series or genre. We also realized that Molly needed a strong talk partner, one who would ask her to prove her thinking by using text evidence, so we changed her reading partner in order to accomplish this. Our ongoing assessment of Molly's reading behavior and habits during independent reading helped to inform our instruction during weekly shared reading, in an effort to move Molly toward independence.

# Bernard: Engaging the Indifferent Reader

Jennifer Lui declared she had an emergency in her fifth-grade classroom. Bernard, a new student to the school, was reading on a second-grade level. Furthermore, Bernard was uninterested in reading during independent work time, and Jennifer was concerned that between his lower reading level and his disinterest in reading itself, Bernard would struggle through fifth grade.

Jennifer had already set up a structure to work specifically with Bernard; after her reading workshop minilesson, she met directly with him or with him and a few other readers and taught another reading strategy or conducted a guided reading group. However, when she left Bernard to read independently, she noticed that he could not sustain the work for more than a few minutes. His eyes roamed the room, often looking longingly at the more sophisticated, interesting texts that his fifth-grade counterparts were reading.

Jennifer and I were committed to finding Bernard texts on a lower reading level that were just as cool as the higher-level texts that permeated his classroom. We scoured book lists and other classrooms, searching for books that might engage Bernard. We offered him these texts, but the time he spent reading them during independent work time was still under five minutes. While Jennifer was extremely thoughtful about how to best support him, Bernard didn't make the progress in reading that she'd hoped for in his fifth-grade year.

As educators, we all have those students who perplex us, who challenge our best teaching practices, who linger on our minds even after the school year is over. Jennifer and I have been thinking about Bernard after his fifth-grade year, wondering how we could have better supported his growth. And then a fifth-grade unit of study in reading workshop sparked an idea.

In this particular unit of study, readers are to read leveled, high-interest short texts in various genres during independent work time. The challenge for the reader, in this unit, is to learn how to quickly assess and identify a text, skillfully employ reading skills to understand the text, and flexibly move from genre to genre. The structure and purpose of this reading workshop unit sound quite similar to those of weekly shared reading.

Since weekly shared reading was in place in Jennifer's classroom, we agreed that her students would have taken well to the challenge of this unit of study. And because reading short, high-interest texts was commonplace in her classroom, there was a better chance that Bernard could have engaged in reading these shorter, varied texts during independent work time. So, we thought, why wait until this unit of study comes around for students like Bernard? Why not have struggling readers read a few short texts (that have been introduced during weekly shared reading) during independent work time?

Jennifer felt that she could have kept her structure of working with Bernard the same, but instead of working with a book he had selected, she could have offered him a variety of short texts to read. Quite purposefully, Jennifer could have offered Bernard texts used in weekly shared reading—texts he would have seen before and worked through with the support of his classmates and teacher. Then it would be Bernard's turn to work through the texts independently and, because he would know the texts well, successfully. Jennifer could push the Bernards—the struggling, unengaged readers in her classroom—into the role of independent, proficient readers; she could provide an experience for these strugglers to *know what it feels like* to read and understand a text independently.

Would Bernard's engagement falter because he had seen the texts before during weekly shared reading, and do other readers lose interest during weekly shared reading because the text is revisited throughout the week? Not necessarily—it's quite the opposite, in most cases. Consider a favorite bedtime story of a toddler, a well-loved book of a kindergartner, a classic novel for a fourth grader; these readers revisit, reread, and rethink texts and books constantly as they build their skills as readers. I think about all the times I've re-read and rethought *Bridge to Terebithia* (Paterson 1977) or *A Tree Grows in Brooklyn* (Smith 1943); I walk away from the text having learned something new, realizing something I hadn't beforehand, and having a deeper appreciation for the characters, story line, and author. Brenda Parkes (2000), author of *Read It Again! Revisiting Shared Reading*, asserts that rereading a text, as part of shared reading, is critical for budding readers:

> Opportunities to return to favorite books, either with an experienced reader or independently, allowed [Sarah] time to savor and experiment with the language and illustrations; to see connections between characters, places, and events in the book and in her world; to make connections to other books; to experiment with the language in her own way; and finally, to make the story her own. (8–9)

Revisiting the texts would have allowed Bernard to make the stories, the facts, and the feelings *his own* as he slowly gained stamina as an independent reader. Bernard could have truly been able to know a text and, through Jennifer's smart teaching, would have been able to more independently practice and apply the essential reading skills needed for full comprehension.

Jennifer reflected on the overall impact of weekly shared reading in her fifth-grade classroom:

> As weekly shared reading became classroom ritual, I was able to watch as my students became increasingly independent and

confident in navigating our weekly text. The explicit focus of each day of the week provided a structure that the students were able to approximate and then practice until it became part of their independent reading lives.

The stories of our struggling readers—Amber, Molly, and Bernard—are both inspirational and perplexing. Through weekly shared reading, Amber began to see herself as a reader, a truly phenomenal feat. Through weekly shared reading, we were able to support Molly as she slowly moved toward independence. And the structure of weekly shared reading sparked an idea that we wished we could have introduced to Bernard. Not only does weekly shared reading have the potential to impact our students as readers, but it also influences our instruction and allows us to be reflective on our practices.

# Ongoing Reflection

Struggling readers are often the emergencies in our classrooms. Once we've pinpointed what challenges these readers face, the goal is to move ahead with targeted, focused instruction. But what *is* that instruction? Is it a program that comes in a box? Is it pullout with the resource room teacher? What interventions work best for our classroom emergencies?

Adele Schroeter, the principal of PS59, often asserts that the most powerful intervention for our classroom emergencies is the classroom teacher herself. No one knows the struggling students as well as she does, and no one is as skilled to provide focused, targeted instruction as she is. The classroom teacher can utilize a variety of structures to meet the needs of her students, including whole-group modeling, small-group instruction, one-on-one conferring, and weekly shared reading.

As a classroom teacher, I took comfort in knowing that weekly shared reading was a structure in my classroom. Daily, I could model the habits of a fluent and proficient reader, return to a familiar text, and invite my struggling students to join in and participate in the meaning-making conversation. Daily, I could assess on the run, listening to my struggling readers' conversations, watching them closely as they stopped and jotted their ideas in their notebooks. Weekly shared reading was another opportunity to assess, to teach, and to assist my struggling readers into a world of reading.

# Big Ideas from Chapter 5

- Weekly shared reading is yet another opportunity for practice of essential reading skills in a supportive setting for the struggling reader.
- Weekly shared reading can allow struggling readers to see themselves as proficient readers, taking on the habits of skilled readers.
- Weekly shared reading can help push nonreaders into a world of reading, positively affecting their independent reading time.
- Through weekly shared reading, students get to know a text well, and struggling readers can deepen their comprehension every time they return to a familiar text.
- Weekly shared reading offers a time for ongoing assessment and reflection, encouraging both student and teacher to be more accountable to learning and teaching.

# Cross-Curricular Reading 6

*Instruction in Content Areas Through Weekly Shared Reading*

Real comprehension has to do with thinking, learning, and expanding a reader's knowledge and horizons. It has to do with building on past knowledge, mastering new information, connecting with the minds of those you've never met.

—SUSAN ZIMMERMAN AND CHRYSE HUTCHINS,
*7 Keys to Comprehension: How to Help Your Kids Read It and Get It!*

Content-area reading can expand our readers' horizons, enrich their vocabulary, and pique their interest in social studies, science, or mathematics. Fortunately, reading in the content areas is prominent in our upper-elementary classrooms. However, in my classroom, I struggled with finding a balance between providing appropriately leveled texts for the required social studies, science, or mathematics scope and sequence and exposing students to more sophisticated, yet engaging texts, which are unfortunately often too challenging for most of my readers. Weekly shared reading was the perfect vehicle for me to talk with my students about a social studies, science, or mathematical concept, expose them to a more challenging text, and still provide them with practice in negotiating complicated text structures.

# Social Studies and Science

Many children who are otherwise good readers have trouble reading science and social studies textbooks. These books often have a table of contents, illustrations with captions, diagrams with labels, maps, charts, a glossary, and an index. Many children do not know what to do when they encounter these foreign elements in their books, so they skip over them. Informational books have different structure and special features that stories don't have. Children must slow down their reading rate and pay attention to more than just the text to comprehend informational books. (Cunningham and Allington 1994, 142)

Social studies and science reading materials present a unique challenge for readers—students must navigate the structure and features of nonfiction while understanding the content and revising their thinking about that content. In this vein, a weekly shared reading text can hold a few purposes—supporting students in working through a more challenging genre and in learning about and having conversations about a pertinent social studies or science topic. I ensure that the social studies or science text isn't too complicated, either structurally or content-wise, because I don't want to overburden my students with either purpose. Lucy Calkins once stated, "Sometimes when you try to kill two birds with one stone, you end up with two dead birds," and I keep this in mind when I select weekly shared reading texts that support my social studies and science curriculum.

When content-rich texts are used in weekly shared reading, I guide students in using comprehension strategies needed to understand informational texts; students practice how to get the maximum information from pictures, maps, charts, graphs, diagrams, and captions (Cunningham and Allington 1994). Through this meaning making, students also learn science and social studies content and vocabulary. The experiences we share as a class during weekly shared reading of social studies or science texts are often recalled during our more formal social studies or science period. In my classroom, I can build on these shared experiences when teaching new content and vocabulary, grounding students' learning in a common context.

## A Social Studies Focus for Weekly Shared Reading

In my fifth-grade classroom, I often chose texts for weekly shared reading that supported my current or future social studies curriculum. I used these texts in my "nonfiction" or "other" slot in my monthlong plan of weekly shared reading. I made sure to include both nonnarrative and narrative texts relating to a particular topic, and I searched for other sources of information from maps, political cartoons, primary source documents, graphs and tables, letters, and graphic organizers. For instance, a primary source document— an advertisement for settlers to buy land in the 1800s—allowed students to practice their reading skills on an unfamiliar genre and text structure, let me be the more skilled other and decode and read aloud the text to my students, and provided an entry point into a conversation about settlers, land purchase, and equity among people during that time period. By building my students' background knowledge through weekly shared reading, I helped them be more able to understand the content discussed in our formal social studies period. They referred back to the advertisement and our conversation as they constructed their understanding of this historical event.

## A Science Focus for Weekly Shared Reading

Learning about the solar system is a rite of passage for many fourth graders. They find this abstract concept so intriguing, yet so elusive and difficult to fully comprehend. Prior to launching this unit of study in my science block, I presented a diagram of the planets, complete with captions and random facts about each one, during weekly shared reading. Hence, a foundation of solar system content and vocabulary emerged as we worked through this text together and squeezed the most information possible out of the diagram and captions. When we entered the formal unit of study on the solar system, all of the students in my classroom had *some* knowledge about this concept, and in turn, more students were able to access the topic. Because students come to our classrooms with a range of backgrounds and experiences, and these traits directly impact their learning, I used the structure of weekly shared reading to give my students a common language before we jumped into our science curriculum.

# A Mathematics Focus for
# Weekly Shared Reading

Catherine Twomey Fosnot and Maarten Dolk (2001) suggest that there is a difference between a "word problem" and a "truly problematic situation" when it comes to educators developing a strong context for students in which they become invested in solving a problem mathematically. The current trend in elementary mathematics is to present "truly problematic situations" to students so they may use what they know and mathematize the problem, arriving at a feasible and reasonable solution. Another truly problematic situation is, however, when students struggle in reading the context problem and in deducing the appropriate information to use to solve it. Another way I can use weekly shared reading to support my students is by working through the *reading and interpretation* of a context problem, leaving the actual solving of the problem for math workshop.

Jennifer Chalfin and I watched her third graders attempt to tackle a context problem in which they were to extend a pattern and form a conclusion about it. We noticed that most of her students had a hard time getting started; they were frozen by the language and demands of the context problem. We were curious to see if working through the reading of a context problem together, during weekly shared reading, would support her learners as both readers and mathematicians.

We selected a context problem and aligned the five essential reading skills with it, carefully thinking about the strategies we would model and encourage our students to try along with us. We were mindful not to jump to solving the context problem; instead we lingered with reading and understanding the *action* of the problem.

Working through this text with the third graders was an eye-opening experience—for both us and them! By slowing the kids down and holding them back from solving the problem mathematically, we were able to help them develop a full understanding of the question posed in the problem and the important information they would need for later. As we transitioned from reading the problem to solving it mathematically, we noticed that students selected more efficient strategies for solving the problem than they had in the past and made fewer errors in their computation. The students told us they felt very confident when it came time to solve the problem; they were sure of their answer because they knew what the problem was asking of them. Jennifer and I realized that by providing the third graders with practice in reading and interpreting a context problem, we had both strengthened their reading skills and addressed their mathematical skills and concept development.

# What Our Nonfiction Readers Can Teach Us

Christine Lagatta, a staff developer from the Teachers College Reading and Writing Project, gathered a few of Wendy Binkowitz's third graders in the meeting area. She had the students open their nonfiction books and take out their sticky notes that they had created in preparation for a discussion. What started out as comical soon turned to unbelievable; the mound of stickies from the four kids on the carpet was embarrassingly large—and the kids were only about a third of the way into their books. Wendy sat in horror, knowing in the back of her mind where she had gone astray. "I taught them to write on stickies," she whispered to me, "but I didn't teach them how to use them as tools to help their understanding."

In the classroom, we often see pieces of our teaching—only parts of the bigger whole. We recognize that students are approximating, attempting to master a particular skill, strategy, or tool. Sometimes, however, kids are stuck in the minutiae, without a context to ground their work. Wendy's kids knew how to sticky: read a little, grab a sticky note, and write *something*. Wendy didn't teach her students to use stickies in this way, of course, but that's what her kids *learned*.

Wendy looked past the sea of yellow notes on the carpet and realized that she had not explicitly shown her students how using sticky notes could help them *synthesize* the text. Her kids were jotting down facts, predictions, and questions on the notes, but they were never using them to make meaning of the text. She had shown them a strategy for deepening their comprehension but had not provided the context—the essential reading and thinking skill of synthesizing.

Her colleague, Barbara, reminded us of Mohammed, the reader of the shark text. Mohammed's book on sharks was peppered with stickies as well, but each note was a restatement of a fact from the text. Mohammed could not tell us what the text was mostly about or share his ideas about sharks.

Our kidwatching allowed us to not only assess our learners but also reflect on our instruction. Our kids weren't truly synthesizing while reading in a variety of genres, and our instruction of the strategies to support synthesizing was not solidly grounded in a context that made sense to our readers. Even though students synthesized during weekly shared reading once a week, we decided to take a closer look at synthesizing and highlight this essential reading skill. We planned to more explicitly model, through think-alouds and demonstrations, what synthesizing looked and sounded like, using phrases and prompts like "I think this is *mostly* about . . ." and "What do you think this all means?" We chose shorter and lower-level non-fiction texts for the next few rounds of weekly shared reading in an effort to provide accessible materials. We also discussed the implications of our assessment and how it would inform our instruction in the other balanced literacy structures in place in our classrooms.

# Ongoing Reflection

It is important to note that weekly shared reading evolves in response to the ongoing instructional needs of our students. Weekly shared reading allows me to introduce new materials and assess understanding in the content areas of social studies, science, and mathematics. While the five-day structure stays in place, there is room to play inside it. What it looks like will change over the course of the week, month, and year. It is a fluid construct designed to build upon the interactions in the classroom. Weekly shared reading changes in response to the type of text, the goal of the day, and the needs of the students.

# Big Ideas from Chapter 6

- Weekly shared reading can support other content areas, such as social studies, science, and mathematics.
- A carefully chosen text may help students develop their schema and vocabulary in a content area.

# Test Preparation

**7**

If our youngsters are accustomed to gathering on the carpet to read a shared, and perhaps enlarged, text together and then talking about strategies for approaching this text or for handling difficulty in this text, why wouldn't they do the same to read an excerpt from a standardized reading test?

—LUCY CALKINS, KATE MONTGOMERY, DONNA SANTMAN, with
BEVERLY FALK, *A Teacher's Guide to Standardized Reading Tests:*
*Knowledge Is Power*

The structure and the method of weekly shared reading lend themselves beautifully to purposeful test preparation. The authors of *A Teacher's Guide to Standardized Reading Tests* (Calkins et al. 1998) suggest that the current, effective structures and methods we have in place in our classrooms—like read-aloud, think-aloud, demonstration, shared reading, guided reading, and conferences—are the same structures and methods teachers should use for instructing children in how to read standardized reading tests. It is often stated that good instruction is good test preparation, yet we know we need to teach our students how to skillfully navigate, read, and understand a reading test before they see it in the spring. Additionally, we work to provide opportunities for our students to read a lot in one sitting;

Richard Allington (2000) suggests that readers, especially struggling ones, need to spend *ninety minutes a day* with their eyes on print. Readers build their stamina for reading by reading during large chunks of time and moving through books at an appropriate pace, and demonstrating stamina while reading greatly assists our students during timed reading tests. Weekly shared reading is another time during the day where all readers have their eyes on print and continue to build their stamina for reading by learning how to actively engage with and have conversations about a text.

# A Variety of Genres

Flip through any standardized reading test and note the different genres throughout—realistic fiction, narrative and nonnarrative nonfiction, poetry, and in some cases, menus, directions, or invitations. While we can encourage our students to read from a variety of genres during reading workshop, we can ensure their exposure to and thinking about various genres during weekly shared reading. As I select texts to use for weekly shared reading, I think about what I know about standardized reading tests and make smart choices about the kinds of texts I share with my students. I utilize the test-preparation materials carefully, picking directions and passages from which I know my students will benefit.

Proficient readers employ the five essential reading skills when they read a passage on a standardized reading test, but they also use smart test-taking skills as well. During weekly shared reading, I make sure to demonstrate both sets of strategies—the reading and thinking strategies that help me make meaning of a text and the test-taking strategies that help me respond to a passage competently. Some of these test-taking strategies include reading the questions at the end of the passage before reading the passage itself, marking up the passage while reading, eliminating choices, and using evidence from the passage to select the best choice.

While weekly shared reading is not intended to serve solely as a time for test preparation, it can support our readers by having them

> 4/15/04
>
> Evan
>
> **What makes up what?**
>
> What makes non-fiction?
>
> • True facts
> • Non-naritive
> • Way in writing like only serious facts.
>
> What makes fiction?
>
> • True and non-true facts or storys
> • Mostly naritive.
> • Mostly false facts.
> • Written in on expressive way as a story.
>
> What makes an Interview?
>
> • A person asking various questions to others.
> • Only about person being questioned.

work through an excerpt from a standardized reading test together,
practicing both reading strategies and test-taking strategies. Additionally, the exposure to different genres through weekly shared reading
will further prepare our students in navigating, reading, and comprehending test passages. In my busy days as an upper-grade educator,
knowing that I can use comfortable structures and methods like
weekly shared reading to support test preparation comforts me and
alleviates my concern about adequately preparing my students for the
reading test while ensuring quality, purposeful instruction.

Figure 7-1b

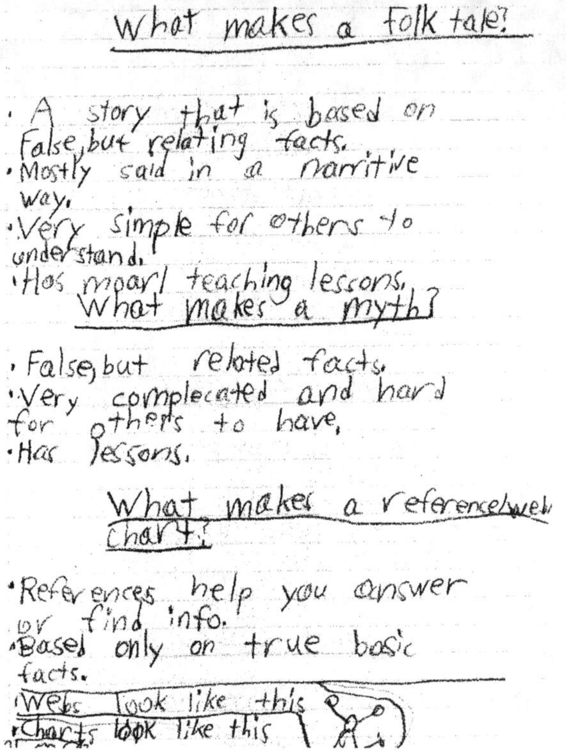

What makes a folk tale?

• A story that is based on false, but relating facts.
• Mostly said in a narritive way.
• Very simple for others to understand.
• Has moarl teaching lessons.

What makes a myth?

• False, but related facts.
• Very complecated and hard for others to have.
• Has lessons.

What makes a reference/web chart?

• References help you answer or find info.
• Based only on true basic facts.
• Webs look like this
• Charts look like this

# A Day-by-Day Account of Weekly Shared Reading: Introducing Third Graders to the Standardized Math Test

In our third-grade classrooms in New York City, the students are asked to take standardized tests for the first time. In addition to being asked to demonstrate their solid grasp of the knowledge, they are confronted with an unfamiliar and challenging genre. In order to make this task a little less overwhelming, the teachers at our school decided to introduce the genre during weekly shared reading. By

Figure 7-1c

Evan                    4/15/04

**What makes Fliers?**
- written in exciting ways.
- always trying to sell or advertise.

**What makes a poem?**
- Rhyems
- Expresses different feelings of emotion.
- Very calming
- lessons
- True or false teachings.

**What makes a bioagraphy?**
- An important person life or sussesful acomplesments writtin books in their own sytle.
- Might teach lessons.

**What makes a Historical article?**
- Talks about historical or life changing things.
- things that happened in the past, a looong time ago.

having a shared conversation, over the course of a week, the students were allowed to delve into this work in a supported setting. They learned how to navigate this complicated genre through teacher modeling; they were able to access their shared background information; they were shown how they are already familiar with many elements of this genre. Weekly shared reading provided these teachers with the ability to model how to read a standardized test, which parts to linger on, and how to differentiate between important and unimportant information.

Jennifer Chalfin's third graders had to take the New York State Third Grade Mathematics Assessment in eight weeks. While Jennifer felt confident about her students' mathematical content knowledge and processes, she knew that it was crucial to teach her kids about the format and structure of the assessment itself. Jennifer planned to spend focused time engaging her students in thoughtful test preparation—looking at the test as a genre—but recognized that through weekly shared reading, she could introduce her students to the format of the test *and* assess her students' understanding and comfort level with the format. Previewing upcoming curriculum through weekly shared reading allows teachers to give their students a heads-up and get them ready to learn new material.

From past assessments, Jennifer anticipated that her students would skillfully preview the text and understand its genre, but they may struggle with visualizing the story problem and experience a breakdown in complete comprehension of the text. In order to help ensure her students' success, she asked me to come into her classroom to introduce a sample extended test question to her students. Jennifer and I chose a page from Book 2 of the Sample Third Grade Math Assessment to use as a text in weekly shared reading (see Figure 7–2). I used weekly shared reading as a tool to strengthen the students' comfort with the genre, so they would be able to focus their attention on the mathematical concepts.

## Day One: First Glance

On Monday, I gathered the students at the meeting area and directed their eyes to the overhead screen.

"Today, we are going to look at a new text. We are going to be looking at it as readers. Every time readers look at a text, they think about what genre it is and what expectations they have for the text," I said.

I turned on the overhead, showing the students a page from a math test. "This text doesn't look familiar to me. It doesn't look like a page from a story. It doesn't look like nonfiction . . . Turn and talk to your partner: what genre do you think this text is?"

I listened in to students' conversations.

"I think it is realistic fiction. It looks like content from the blurb," said Cedric.

"It looks like a math problem," Charlie said.

"What makes this genre look like a math problem?" I asked.

"It looks like a pattern. We had something like this for homework once," Ariana said.

"I see the word *answer*" Sam said.

Figure 7–2    The sample question: item 28

**28**    Luis counts the total number of ducks swimming on a pond each day. On Monday, he counts 1 duck. On Tuesday, he counts 2 ducks. On Wednesday, he counts 4 ducks. On Thursday, he counts 8 ducks.

**Part A**

If the pattern continues, how many ducks will Luis count on Saturday?

*Show your work.*

*Answer* _____ ducks

**Part B**

On the lines below, describe the pattern you used to find your answer.

_____

_____

_____

_____

_____

Page 6                            Book 2                        ■ Sample Test 2005 ■

"I see *Part A* and *Part B*," Danyil said.

"So, now that we know it is a math problem, what are we expecting to have in it? Turn and talk to your partner," I said.

I then listened in to conversations.

"I can expect a story—a story problem," said Cedric.

"There will be a situation," John said.

"Numbers," Reem said.

"Numbers and words," Theoren said.

"Writing. The lines make me think I have to write there," Sam said.

"Great thinking, readers. Now we are going to read it," I said. "I came across a situation and numbers. Hmm . . . we didn't say, 'Question.' I see a question, 'How many ducks will Luis count on Saturday?' So, whenever you look at a math problem, you can expect a situation, numbers, or something you have to work with. Tomorrow, we are going to focus on what information we need to know and what we don't need to know. Great work today."

Over the course of ten minutes, I was able to introduce the students to this new genre—the math test. I encouraged the students to participate in this investigatory work, to realize that they already knew a lot about this genre. The students are eased into this work, are given a chance to dip their feet in. In the course of ten minutes, the kids identified what a math test can look like. We now had a list: math tests have situations, numbers, sections, questions, and lines. Instead of telling them the elements of the genre, I supported them in figuring it out.

## Day Two: Doing a Double Take

On Tuesday, to help students locate themselves in this math problem, I focused on the reading strategy of determining importance in a text. (This genre lends itself to separating the important information from the extraneous information.) I invited the students to the rug and began: "Readers, yesterday when we took a first glance at this text, we focused on its genre and our expectations as a reader. We decided it was a math problem and that we expect to get information from it to solve the problem. We saw that there are words, numbers, a work section, and lines for writing. So, now we know we have a purpose for reading this problem—to solve it. Readers always ask themselves, 'Why am I reading this?'

"Today we are going to focus on what information is important and what is not so important, knowing that our reason for reading it is to solve the problem. When readers find important information, they mark up the text. Sometimes they underline text, sometimes they put a star. Watch me as I start reading" I read, "Luis counts the total number of ducks swimming on a pond each day. On Monday, he counts one duck.' Hmm . . . 'Monday,' 'one duck,' that's important. I am going to underline *Monday* and *one duck*."

I kept reading, "'On Tuesday, he counts two ducks . . . Hmm . . . 'Tuesday,' two ducks.'" I underlined *Tuesday* and *two ducks*.

Helena raised her hand. "I notice that on Monday there's one duck. On Tuesday, there are two. The number doubles."

"I notice you're looking at it as a mathematician," I acknowledged before returning to my reading and underlining. "Wednesday equals four ducks. Thursday equals eight ducks," I said as I underlined both. "So as readers, it looks like we are noticing a pattern. That's really important. OK, now it's your turn. Look at the rest of the page—Part A and Part B. What are you going to mark up? Turn and talk to your partner." I started to move around the classroom, listening to conversations.

"A lot of you said to underline *Saturday*. This is all going to help us solve the problem. What else is important?"

"*If the pattern continues* (in Part A)," said Stephanie.

"*Describe the pattern* (in Part B). You wouldn't know what to write for this section without the information," Sloan said.

"Great," I said, "because we set a purpose for reading we (1): know to continue the pattern to Saturday and (2) know to describe the pattern. Knowing the important information helps us know what our work is as a reader and a mathematician. Tomorrow, we are going to work on visualizing the problem. Great work today readers!"

I encouraged the students to focus on the math problem as readers first and foremost, and modeled how to determine and note important information needed to solve the problem. Depending upon the need, the teacher's involvement and level of instruction will change. On Monday, I had more of a supporting role. I asked guiding questions, but the students really owned the conversation. On Tuesday, though, I chose to spend a lot more time on instruction.

## Day Three: Filling in the Picture

For Wednesday, Jennifer and I decided to focus on a different reading skill—envisioning the story problem. Jennifer knew that traditionally this skill had been challenging for her students and was curious to see how they would fare during this lesson. Since she wanted her students to quickly sketch the situation, she provided each student with a copy of the text and passed out clipboards and pencils. She asked me to lead one more day before she took the reins.

I began, "Readers, I know you are ready to switch hats and to solve this problem like a mathematician. But we still have work to do as readers. Today's work is going to be visualizing the story problem. This will help us understand what's going on in the story. When we read our fiction books, we picture the story in our mind. Most of our books don't have a lot of pictures, so we have to visualize what's happening in our mind. This work can be done in math as well.

"Today, we are going to visualize this math story problem and sketch the images we see in our mind. One strategy I like to use when I picture something in my mind is a quick sketch. So, as I am reading, I am going to quickly sketch the details of the problem."

Then I started reading and slowly modeling. I wrote:

| Mon. | Tues. |
|------|-------|
| X | XX |

"I didn't draw ducks because that would take too long. One *X* means one duck. It is easier to record this way. Now it's your turn. I am going to continue reading the problem, and you can quickly sketch how it will continue." I read and the kids sketched. I circled around to see the kids' work.

I then shared their thinking on the overhead.

| Wed. | Thurs. |
|------|--------|
| XXXX | XXXX |
| | XXXX |

"I like to set up quick sketches in a way that's easy for me; I know four plus four equals eight.

"Let's continue to visualize the ducks and how they change day by day." I kept reading. "So, we have to continue the pattern and think about how many you'll have on Friday. Hmmm . . . continue to quickly sketch the pattern for Friday." I walked around and observed.

"I see lots of numbers here for Friday." I read from the story problem again. "On Monday, one; on Tuesday, two; on Wednesday, four. So, the numbers don't go in order. Hmmm . . . I'm visualizing the ducks. There are more ducks each day. How many were there on Friday?"

"Sixteen because 1 plus 1 is 2 and 2 plus 2 is 4 and 4 plus 4 is 8 and 8 plus 8 is 16," Charlie said.

"So, they are doubling. Now, do a quick sketch for Saturday," I said. Kids began sketching. I walked around.

"Reem, what's happening every day? It's doubling, so you have two, four, eight, and sixteen. What would come next?" I asked as I conferred with Reem.

I noticed kids were using *X's* and tallies. "What do you do to extend the pattern? *Extend* means continue."

"You double sixteen," Ariana said.

I noticed Danyil had continued to Sunday. "Do you extend the pattern to Sunday?"

"No!" said the kids.

"Right . . . if I go back to the important information, it stops at Saturday," I said. "So, readers, when you are reading a math problem, you need to visualize and read what you have to do to solve the problem. Tomorrow, we are going to look at Part B, and Friday you will do all the math work. Good work today, third graders!"

By modeling all of the thinking work that needed to be done before even attempting to solve a problem, I let the students know that the expectation was to *slow it down*. I showed them all of the reading work that needed to be done before they approached this problem as mathematicians. Week after week, the kids learn that regardless of what the genre is, they should take the time to really soak it in before reacting.

## Day Four: Digging Deeper

One of the process standards in mathematics proposes that students make connections between problems, strategies used in problems, and problems and real life. This work suggests that students infer and think beyond the text when they read a story problem. On Thursday, Jennifer took on the task of modeling this challenging work.

"Readers, yesterday we left off on Part A of the text. We worked to visualize the story problem and used a quick sketch to fill in the picture. This has put us in a good position to solve this problem. But we still have important reading work to do. Today we're going to look at Part B, reading carefully and thinking beyond the text," Jennifer said.

"Part B states: 'On the lines below, describe the pattern you used to find your answer.' A few days ago, it was pointed out that 'describe the pattern' was an important part of the text to remember. I have it marked right here on the page!

"When I read, 'describe the pattern,'" Jennifer continued, "I need to think beyond this particular text to other times when I have described a pattern. This is math work I've done before. Turn and talk—when have you done this math work before?"

Jennifer listened in to partnership conversations. Many students were talking about geometric patterns they had extended and could describe.

"Eyes up! Many of you talked about the geometric patterns you created with pattern blocks and described those patterns like 'blue rhombus, two green triangles, one yellow hexagon, and back to the blue rhombus . . .' You can use the same language to describe a numerical pattern like the one here with the ducks. When readers read a text, they are always thinking beyond the text, trying to relate the information they are reading to information they already know. The clues in the text help them make this connection. So, the clues in this text, 'describe the pattern,' allowed us to think beyond this text and recall times when we've described patterns."

"So," said Jennifer, "can you turn and talk with a partner and describe this pattern using the numbers in the problem?"

"The numbers of ducks double every day," Ariana said.

"On the first day, there's one duck, then on the second day, there are two ducks, et cetera," Danyil said.

"Readers, I heard you using very precise mathematical terms to describe this pattern. Just like you can describe a geometric pattern, you can describe a numerical pattern. Good readers always think beyond the text to deepen their understanding of the text itself, and today we did that by thinking of connections to other math problems where we've done the same kind of work," said Jennifer.

As Jennifer listened to partnership conversations, she heard many of her students talking about geometric patterns they had extended and could describe. This seemed natural; third graders can picture concrete geometric shapes and colors more so than numbers.

Demystifying terminology used on the test by reminding students that they have already done work like this before can empower students and build their testing confidence.

## Day Five: Getting the Big Picture

On Friday, Jennifer wanted to slowly release ownership of the text to the students. In contrast to the beginning of the week, when I was providing more scaffolding to support student understanding by modeling and demonstrating, Jennifer now offered her students "lean prompts" and guided them through the synthesizing process with their partners. She wanted to confirm that her readers fully understood this story problem before they tried to answer it mathematically. She gently guided them in synthesizing the text, ensuring that they understood all the separate parts of the text *and* the text as a whole.

"Readers," Jennifer began, "before we put on our mathematician hats, we need to check in with ourselves to make sure that we understand all parts of the text *and* what the whole text is mostly about."

"So," she continued, "let's think about this part [*pointing to the first section of the text*] and say what it's about in just a few words. Turn and talk with your partner." Jen listened in to student conversations.

"Let's look at Part A. What's this about, in just a few words? Turn and talk." Jennifer listened in to student conversations.

"And now, the last part, Part B. Again, turn and talk with your partner. What's this section about?" Jennifer listened as the students talked.

"Now readers, take a step back from each of these parts, and let's think about the text as a whole. What's this *all* mostly about, in just a few words? Turn and talk."

Jennifer noticed that her students could easily summarize the three parts of the text, but had a more difficult time synthesizing those parts together and thinking about the big ideas of the entire text. As Jennifer listened to partnership conversations, she led some students to generalize the bigger idea of the text, understanding and extending patterns. She shared this bigger idea with the entire group.

"So now readers, you have a very deep understanding of this math story problem, and you are ready to solve this problem with your mathematician hats on! So, let's make that transition, and using everything that you've learned this week about this problem, solve it accurately and completely."

As the weekly shared reading session morphed into five-minute math, Jen knew that her students had definitely benefited from this introduction to the format and structure of the math test and would be better prepared to read story problems with deeper understanding.

# Jennifer's Ongoing Reflection

A thoughtful educator, Jennifer was reflective throughout this whole process. She was constantly thinking about how to best meet her students' needs. At the beginning of this process, she said:

> I looked at my students during math workshop and our morning "do nows" [the work students do when they enter the classroom in the morning] and saw their strong understanding of numerous mathematical concepts and processes. They all seemed to grasp the units I had taught them, some with the support of visuals and manipulatives. But, then as I began test preparation, I saw some of my strongest mathematicians struggle with math test questions. I saw them at times choose the wrong operation, not see the two-step part, or misunderstand what the problem was asking them to do. I only saw some students apply the strategies I had taught them during ELA, such as underlining key phrases, looking at all the answers, reading and rereading the directions, [and so on . . . I really started realizing the importance of teaching them to look at the math test as a genre—looking at it as a reader, then a mathematician.

Jen was constantly thinking about her own practice—what she could do in order to best support her students. After introducing weekly shared reading into her own classroom, she shared:

> It was important for them to see the overall structure and organization of the problem. Most of them recognized it being a math problem, because they have seen a lot of story problems before. But they were not used to seeing Part A and B as well as space constraints. They are more used to having a problem, then a

large box or space to work in. Many of my kids take things literally as well as some have organizational difficulties, so [it] helped them take a glance to see where to put all their work, especially with the need of expressing their thinking in words, numbers, and pictures. Previewing helps many of my kids feel confident and comfortable with approaching a problem.

By having her students preview the text, she was able to begin to see where the disconnect was. Furthermore, it helped to have her students observe me as I slowed the process down; they were able to think about how the text was set up, to take it all in.

On day two, the students were able to observe me as I approached the problem. It helped to have a teacher show *all the work* that goes into solving a problem. Jen reflected,

After seeing the problem once already, it was good to model how to determine information needed to solve the problem. Physically showing them how to mark up the text is so important for my kids. They transfer what they see during a think-aloud into their independent work in all subjects. It was also important to say that underlining is one way to mark up a text; a star is another, since some kids might have their own method. Since this problem skipped Friday and asked for Saturday, that was an important focus! Again, many of my students tend to read too quickly or don't read into things (they have literal interpretation), so that is something they will now look out for.

Many students don't even know where to start when solving a word problem. Word problems can be so tricky! It helped Jen's students to have me break the context problem down.

On day three, I modeled how to solve the problem. Jen reflected:

I think this is the most important lesson of the week. I am such a visual learner and so are many of my students. Some try to start solving a problem using numbers without truly visualizing and understanding the problem. Modeling the use of $X$s is so effective because without modeling, some kids would take time drawing ducks. As they were sketching, you could tell how they began picking up the problem right away.

It was also a great way for me to assess the kids. Many of them wrote their $X$s in an organized way (by twos or fours) for it to be a quick image to them for future use.

The organization of Mon. Tues. [and so on] also helped them make a connection to visually seeing a calendar, which they do on a daily basis.

Both Jen and her students benefited from taking the time to break this work down into smaller steps. Weekly shared reading affords students with different learning styles access to a problem. In this case, visual learners were able to really see the work that went into solving the problem.

On day four, Jen said:

> This was important because the kids are always making connections while reading. This gave them the opportunity to think about all the other times we've done pattern work in math as well as art. It allowed them the opportunity to use precise math language, which is necessary for them to use when they share their mathematical thinking on the test.

Creating a community of learners lets the kids build on each other's ideas. They can hear the different strategies, the different entry points. Weekly shared reading allows for shared knowledge.

On day five, Jen reflected:

> This was a nice way to end so they could see how all the work during the week will help them overall solve a math problem. We did so much work with "mostly about" during ELA test prep, that it was important for them to think about the big picture when approaching a math problem. It also allows them to think big when they go ahead and solve the problem, because then they will think, "Does my answer make sense, now that I really know the problem?"

What once seemed overwhelming, was no longer. The students felt a sense of accomplishment. Their deep understanding of both the problem and the work it takes to solve a word problem evolved over the course of the week. The mystique surrounding a word problem dissipated as the kids worked together to solve the problem.

Jen shares her final thoughts:

> After implementation of the week's shared reading, my kids showed an amazing turnaround. When I observed them doing test-prep problems, they focused on reading and rereading the problem, they marked up the text, and sketched pictures to make sure they understood the problem. When they took a mock day two booklet, twenty out of twenty-one students got a problem similar to the one used during the shared reading component entirely correct. Four students in the class got full

credit on every problem of the booklet. Sixteen others showed the ability to get at least a Level 3, if not a 4, on day two. They all showed confidence, applying not only their mathematical knowledge but also their understanding of the genre.

Since Jennifer knew that none of her students had seen a standardized math test before, she was able to introduce them to this "new world" during weekly shared reading. Over the course of a week, she and I were able to show them how to navigate this somewhat daunting task. We gave the students the language and the tools that enabled them to successfully take on this new challenge. Weekly shared reading allows teachers to introduce students to test-preparation materials in a supportive environment and in a familiar and predictable structure.

# Big Ideas from Chapter 7

- Standardized tests are packed with a variety of genres, and students need to know how to navigate those various genres within a limited time frame.
- Weekly shared reading can support thoughtful test preparation. Students can practice reading skills and test-taking skills on a shared text.
- The chosen shared texts reflect the needs of the students; if it seems as if students need more time unpacking a certain type of text, weekly shared reading can be planned accordingly.

# Anecdotes and Reflections from the Field

## Empowering Students to Find Their Own Voices

The power of weekly shared reading comes from our interactions. While it starts off small—ten to fifteen minutes a day over the course of a week—the work we do creates a foundation that weaves its way throughout our days, weeks, months, and years. Our interactions during weekly shared reading grow into an ongoing class dialogue that provides all of my students access to the same conversation; encourages students to think within and across different genres; allows for an additional opportunity to support and assess; and ultimately deepens my students' thinking, reading, and writing work.

In this chapter, I often refer to "we." Weekly shared reading builds on the ideas of *all of the members* of our classroom. Obviously, in September, the initial onus is on me, the teacher. I model the expectations, letting the students know how to return to and engage with a text over the course of a week. As the days and weeks go on, though, there is a shift. I encourage the students to take on a more participatory role. Our interactions fluidly move between student and student and teacher and student. By the spring, the students take a leading role in the conversation. While I choose the texts, they help decide how the conversation goes and grows. This structure provides *all of my students* with access to an ongoing conversation, encouraging my students to find their own voices.

As the year goes on, the students realize that during weekly shared reading we have the time and the space to return to something we touched on earlier in the week, month, or year. Through this work, my students begin to realize that there are some common threads within a genre. They see connections *within and across* genres. In order to accomplish this, I show my students how to

- return to a text again and again
- look at a text in different ways over the course of a week
- build upon our ideas earlier in the week, month, and/or year
- build on what was taught during reading or writing instruction
- access and build upon prior knowledge
- preview what is yet to be taught
- use what was taught during weekly shared reading in their independent work

This scaffolded support helps them deepen their own reading and pushes their own writing further.

Weekly shared reading affords me with the opportunity to teach all of my students how to claim their voices in our learning community. Often, I find that only certain students' voices are clear from the moment they walk in my door. Those students, through opportunities and personalities, have formed their voices—they feel comfortable sharing their thoughts and themselves with those around them. The beauty of weekly shared reading is that it encourages the quieter voices to contribute to the ongoing classroom conversation. Because weekly shared reading is a collaborative structure, the spotlight isn't on individual children, and I find that frequently unheard voices slowly and comfortably enter into our conversation.

I have found that weekly shared reading has helped the students at PS59 move away from teacher-led instruction toward student independence. In May, when Arlinda showed me her literary essay (full of the fingerprints of the work we'd done during weekly shared reading), I knew this extra structure in our busy day had been worthwhile. I had been able to provide her with a support system designed to move her toward independence. Now, I invite you to our classroom. I invite you to listen into our conversations.

## Deepening Our Students' Work—Building upon What They Already Know

It was May in my classroom and the class was looking at a *Time for Kids* article, "An Immigrant Nation" (Satterfield 2006). I wanted to remind the kids that at this time in the year, they could really focus on having their genre expectations confirmed as opposed to identifying the features of the genre.

SARAH: Readers, our shared reading of the week is this: *Time for Kids* [*shows the front page on the overhead*] and this is the actual page we are going to be reading: "An Immigrant Nation" [*shows the article on the overhead*].

[*Returns to the front page*] At this time in the year, I feel as if we're pretty familiar with genres. So even if we're looking at something on a Monday, we know what the genre looks like—the characteristics of it. So today what I thought we could really think about is confirming what we know about the genre.

[*Already, on a dry-erase board, Sarah has written, "An Immigrant Nation: Having a First Glance."*]

In your head, I want you to take a second to think about it. If you're seeing this nonfiction article [*shows the actual article*], what are your expectations for it? What are you looking for? What are you expecting to see? When you have some ideas, put your thumb up . . . So I'm waiting for quiet thumbs . . . Most of you have your thumbs up, so let's start.

ABHINAV: Bold words—words that mean a lot to the story. Bold words that have to do a lot with the story.

SARAH: OK, so more than it even being words where you might need a definition, it's bold because they're important and you have to know them. [*Sarah writes "Bold Words" on the dry-erase board.*]

AIDAN: It's literally bold, but it's like bold because it's important.

SARAH: So, they're highlighted because they're important. [*Sarah adds on, "Highlighted because they are important."*]

CLAIRE: I was also thinking about the bold words. 'Cause this is like a kids' magazine, so they have big words. So they bold all of the big words that kids might not know.

SARAH: So you're saying that knowing it's a kids' magazine—more than it being nonfiction, but nonfiction for kids—they're going to do that. We can expect that . . . so

I'm going to write that up there. [*Sarah adds on, "It's not just that it's nonfiction, it's nonfiction for kids. So our expectations are going to be different."*] . . . That's an interesting point.

In this section of the lesson, we see that while I guided my students through this conversation, my role was more of a facilitator than a participant. I reiterated what my students said, clarified what they were talking about, but really it is the students who did the deep work. They built upon their classmates' ideas. They pushed each other to say more, to think thoughtfully about an idea as tiny as bold words.

As the conversation went on, the students both confirmed their expectations and demonstrated their deep understanding of this genre.

SARAH: Other things? Anthony?

ANTHONY: Using pictures to show what they were trying to say.

SARAH: [*Pointing to picture in text*] So, it seems like your expectations were confirmed. [*I write, "Pictures show what they are trying to say."*]
Other people? Reese?

REESE: It's about a serious matter.

SARAH: So your thinking is that it was going to be about a serious matter. [*I add this to the list.*] In this case, was it confirmed?

REESE: Yes.

SARAH: [*Aidan raises his hand.*] Aidan?

AIDAN: I thought there would be quotes because in nonfiction —sometimes — there are a lot of quotes. And there . . . [*pointing to the screen*] it says, "George Bush said" . . . and then blah, blah, blah.

SARAH: Where it had him talking . . . [*pointing to the overhead*] . . . OK, here . . . at the end. [*Aidan nods.*] So, you're thinking that when you're reading nonfiction there are going to be quotes in it. [*I add this idea to the ongoing list.*]

AIDAN: Yeah.

OSKANA: Um, can you go back to the front page?

SARAH: Yeah, sure. I like that you are thinking about that.

OSKANA: I kind of, like, knew that "A Battle over the Border . . . How should the U.S. have handled people who have entered the country illegally? Lawmakers are fighting it out" [*the caption on the cover*] . . . It kind of, like, shows you what is this all about.

SARAH: So you're going to expect that there will be a caption or title that will show you what this is all about when you look at the front page, when you're reading?

OSKANA: Yeah.

SARAH: [*Writes, "Title/caption is set up to show you what it's all about"*]

In this part of the conversation, Oskana took the lead. She smartly reminded both me and her classmates of the importance of returning to the cover page. Within the structure of weekly shared reading, there is a certain level of flexibility in terms of who is in charge of the conversation. Within this structure, I was able to create an environment where the kids were encouraged to take charge, where I was not seen as the sole keeper of knowledge. These students knew that this was a shared conversation, where their perspectives and insights were a valued part of the ongoing dialogue. Not only did this help the conversation to grow, but it allowed me to deepen my understanding of what the students knew. Oskana, for example, moved to the United States a year earlier, and at that time she did not speak a word of English. Now she demonstrated that she not only knew how to participate in this type of conversation, but she understood the value of lifting the level of her classmates' thinking.

As the conversation went on, my students demonstrated their higher-level thinking about this genre.

ELIANA: I thought that there would be a title and other subtitles, breaking it up into sections.

SARAH: Can you show me where that ended up happening?

ELIANA: Yeah, right in the middle column where it says, "Dreaming of America."

SARAH: Nice, great. Expectations that you had that were confirmed. [*Adds Eliana's thinking to the list*]

COLLETTE: The titles are bold too.

SARAH: So you think that is another reason the titles are bold—aside from it being a definition—is that it can also be to let the reader know what it's mostly about. Interesting.

Kate?

KATE: I've read other *Time for Kids* before . . . and based on what you said to think about expectations, I kind of thought about graphs . . . because they usually have graphs that show information. It was kind of proved on the bottom right . . . [*I point to a pie chart on the page.*]

SARAH: So you know that when you're reading nonfiction that it has graphs to help you understand it, and that was confirmed. Your thinking?

KATE: 'Cause for some kids, to look at something visually is easier. Like I know that it helps me. Some kids like to look at something visual, so you can actually see.

SARAH: [*I add Kate's thinking to the chart.*]

Great, I'm just going to take two more hands. Yeah, Derek.

DEREK: Well, at first, when I was talking to Jaime, I was thinking, "Why didn't they put an interview with an immigrant?" But then I was thinking they're illegal here. How are they going to figure out? And if they did find them, they might send them back to where they came from.

SARAH: So, you're thinking about the story that's being told and how that is going to make the author decide whom he or she should put in it. That's a really interesting point that you're bringing up. The voices that you're going to hear are based on the story being told. The author is talking about immigrants, about how they may be illegal. They may not want their story told right now because they might get in trouble. So you're thinking about the author's story and how that influences who is interviewed.

Tiffany?

| | |
|---|---|
| TIFFANY: | I sort of expected it to be set up in columns, as opposed to a story. |
| SARAH: | Why did you have that expectation? |
| TIFFANY: | Because usually if it's an article, a newspaper or something, they usually have it in columns. |
| SARAH: | [*Writes down Tiffany's thinking*]<br><br>At this point in the year, we're moving beyond Mondays just being about identifying the genre. We're thinking about the ideas we have about a genre. We have ideas about what nonfiction looks like. And we should be thinking whether or not this confirms what we expected. |

Without direct instruction, these students went beyond superficial genre identification and moved toward thoughtful conversations about the author's motive, the text setup, and so on. My students demonstrated that they had internalized the five essential reading skills, that they had moved into the metacognitive work encouraged by the weekly shared reading structure.

Even though the nonfiction unit of study took place in November, through weekly shared reading, I was able to continually assess what my students knew about this genre. I was able to get a sense of what they retained, to see what they might have learned on their own, and to realize that by continually returning to nonfiction pieces once a week every month, weekly shared reading deepened my students' understanding of this genre.

## Overcoming Assumptions Through Weekly Shared Reading

In my fifth-grade classroom, the weekly shared reading text of the week was a poem in which the author compared a flower to a person. After reading the poem aloud, I asked my students to turn and talk about what they saw in their mind's eye.

| | |
|---|---|
| SARAH: | I'm picturing a gardenia. Turn and talk to your partner —what did you picture? |
| ANTHONY: | I pictured . . . the kind of flower you would see in grocery stores. |

I imagined the luscious flowers that my grandfather grew in his suburban garden. Based on my experience, that was the image that came to mind, the type of flower I imagined many of my children would mention. To my surprise, Anthony thought of the flowers one buys in a deli. Upon reflection, it made total sense, but it was not at all what I had anticipated. As a student growing up in New York City, Anthony was not going to have the same experience as someone growing up in Rhode Island.

Anthony's response—that one tiny moment—was so key. As a teacher, it reminds me of the power of weekly shared reading conversations. By having time for an extended, shared dialogue, I am able to bring to light my students' different perspectives and allow the members of my classroom (including myself) to learn from each other. I am reminded that my students' engagement with the world will look different depending upon their individual experiences.

In much the same way as one's home or school experiences might affect one's worldview, our students' various socioeconomic backgrounds will affect their perspectives. In *Unequal Childhoods: Class, Race, and Family Life,* Annette Lareau (2003) argues that there is a clear distinction between the values imparted by parents from middle-class and working-class and poor backgrounds. Through nine case studies of families from different socioeconomic backgrounds, she illuminates "the largely invisible but powerful ways that parents' social class impacts children's life experiences . . . For working-class and poor families, the cultural logic of child rearing at home is out of synch with the standards of institutions" (3). She is clear to point out that that doesn't mean that the middle-class approach is *the* approach, just that it provides certain advantages for children when they are asked to engage with larger societal institutions.

I often find myself thinking about what this means for my students. While it seems that some of my students naturally excel, I know that it is often because their parents' home-rearing practices match those of the school setting. For children from working-class and poor families, there is often a split between their home culture and their school culture. As a result, certain children are at a distinct disadvantage in school. While I might not agree with those dominant values, I need to remember that I should give all my students the opportunity to have equal footing within the classroom. I need to ask myself, How can I provide *all of my students* access to the dominant cultural values? Am I providing all of my students with the opportunity to successfully navigate these different worlds? Am I finding opportunities to access home knowledge? Am I creating an environment where different perspectives are welcomed?

It is important that educators find ways to introduce our students to unfamiliar experiences, to new ways of thinking. I hope that weekly shared reading, in some small way, can be used as a tool to provide shared access. If I provide a window into these different worlds for kids, then I can potentially provide them with cultural capital.

There might be certain texts, like a sample math test, that I need to introduce to the whole class. There might be other texts that I choose because they open the eyes of my students to new experiences. I need to continually reconsider where my students are coming from and what I'm teaching. Am I making assumptions? Am I challenging them? Am I truly valuing their prior knowledge? I need to ask myself what I can do to expand my students' horizons. Sometimes, I do not always remember to consider all of these factors. The beauty of weekly shared reading is that it encourages these varied perspectives to come to light.

Through our weekly shared reading dialogues, I am able to develop an understanding of what my students have or have not been exposed to. I am able to use this information to inform my planning—to think about how to push our collective thinking. With weekly shared reading, we can help each other navigate our different worlds.

# Ongoing Reflection

The deeper I delve into this work, the more I appreciate that weekly shared reading grows out of the words, thoughts, and ideas of *all of the members of our community*. It is our collective thinking that is the crux of this work.

My students' varied experiences inform the types of conversations we have, oftentimes allowing us to travel down unexpected paths. It is essential that I remember that this is a *shared process*. Not only do my students end up teaching each other new things, but I benefit as well—I develop a deeper sense of what they know and have a better idea of where to go next.

# Big Ideas from Chapter 8

- Weekly shared reading is a powerful vehicle to create and sustain shared classroom experiences through conversation.
- Students build on their current knowledge and understanding through hearty conversations around shared texts; the teacher facilitates these conversations.
- Practitioners can expose their students to particular ideas through culturally and socially diverse texts. Impacting the citizens of our country is a hefty responsibility, and literature lends itself to opening our students' eyes.

# A Schoolwide Initiative 9

*Beyond My Classroom to Our Collaborative Work*

I love to visit classrooms—to revel in the "hum" of students at work, in conversations, reading, writing, mathematizing. As I walk down our upper-grade hallway, I peer into classrooms and walk in, sliding up to a child for a conference or watching masterful teaching.

I recall walking by a colleague's room to find it dark, which was unusual. My first reaction, judging by the deep focus of the students, was that they were watching a movie. I was perplexed—we often save movie watching for indoor recess—so I peered in the window. I then realized that the students were fixated on an enlarged, beautiful text, projected from the overhead. The teacher was sitting by the overhead, pointing out various parts of the map, which illuminated the room. And then I realized, once again, the power and possibilities of weekly shared reading.

—Adele Schroeter, principal, PS59

# A Learning Community: Pushing Professional Inquiry

The power of professional inquiry can transform a school; teachers feel like they are a part of the bigger conversation—a part of creating new thinking and generating systemic change. Professional inquiry allows for practitioners to experience some ownership of ideas and the plan, and it increases the chance that an initiative will be adopted and implemented. A top-down mandated program or practice is often met with resistance and skepticism from practitioners, while a staff-generated idea is often excitedly embraced.

Professional inquiry grows from the solid, supportive roots of a true learning community. A sustained focus on teaching and learning can transform a school into a learning community; principals set and maintain this focus through thoughtful decision making. Principals who are true instructional leaders model lifelong learning for their staff. They are involved in principal study groups, attend conferences, visit each other's schools, and peruse professional literature. They beckon the experts to come and work with them, their staff, and their students in the hopes that everyone will become smarter about how to learn.

The focus on teaching and learning at PS59 sparked collaborative partnerships between colleagues. Teachers, along with our instructional leadership team, worked together tirelessly to ensure instruction matched students' needs. Teachers' voices were important and valid. As a member of this productive, supportive environment, one could feel safe in taking risks, in asking questions, and in celebrating successes.

It was in this learning community at PS59 where the idea of weekly shared reading grew from reflection, to professional inquiry, to an upper-grade initiative. The learning environment sustained the inquiry, the instructional leadership encouraged the wondering, and the staff took the risk in implementing the practice.

# The Power of Reflection

In the hectic school day—with students and after students leave—there doesn't seem to be enough time to do it all, especially reflect on teaching practices and student learning. However, developing a reflective practice is crucial for effective instruction, and reflecting is one of the best uses of a teacher's precious time.

It is during these moments of reflection—whether after school in a quiet classroom, in the shower, or on the commute home—that *aha!* moments occur. The *aha!* moments can transform a classroom, transform teaching practice, transform student learning and achievement. In the fading sunlight on a May afternoon, Sarah had an *aha!* moment that spurred a schoolwide initiative that would support upper-grade readers in a systematic and powerful way.

While every *aha!* moment won't lead educators to an upper-grade initiative, it will lead to better instructional decisions that clearly align with students' needs. To grow professionally, taking time to reflect on our practice is fundamental; to help more students learn, taking time to reflect on our practice is nonnegotiable.

# The Power of Conversation and Collaboration

Although learning is a social process, we can, ironically, often feel isolated and alone as practitioners. Most of us are the only adult in our classroom throughout the day. Our students challenge and inspire us to create new thinking about instruction, and sharing that thinking with our colleagues only augments our ideas. Through conversation and collaboration, we are enlightened and encouraged by our colleagues' input, suggestions, and thinking. Scheduling is a difficult task for school building leadership, but it is imperative that grade-level colleagues have common planning times throughout the week. The leadership team in a building seeks to foster collaboration and communication among its teachers, and structuring time for grade-level teachers to talk, plan, look at student work, and wonder will do just that.

Some schools are fortunate to have an in-house literacy coach; some have districtwide literacy coaches. Either way, a literacy coach can host the conversations that impact instructional practices and student learning. Among the myriad responsibilities of a literacy coach, teaching literacy content knowledge and pedagogical content knowledge is a key role (Casey 2006). An effective literacy coach, rooted in sound teaching practices, can guide implementation of a schoolwide literacy initiative.

As teacher and literacy coach, we—Sarah and Maria, respectively—began to brainstorm what weekly shared reading, as it is now known, would look like to most effectively support upper-grade readers as they navigated more sophisticated texts, genres, and ideas. We reflected on the work we had done with readers throughout our teaching careers; we discussed the current thinking on teaching instruction and assessment; we researched and read books and articles written by educators and reading instructors; we hypothesized and wondered. Thinking grew out of our conversations; we were brimming with ideas that we couldn't wait to propose to our upper-grade colleagues.

# The Power of a Learning Community

Both our principal, Adele Schroeter, and our instructional superintendent, Leslie Zackman, were intrigued by and very supportive of our idea for an upper-grade initiative. They encouraged us to plan, to pull potential shared reading texts, and to begin the conversation with our upper-grade colleagues. They committed professional development time for us to discuss the rationale behind weekly shared reading and eventually implement it.

With the support of our instructional leadership team, we posed our thinking to our upper-grade colleagues. Not surprisingly, they too were curious about how to more effectively and powerfully push their readers through sophisticated texts. We designed three professional development sessions around weekly shared reading. With the help of our third-grade colleague, Barbara Rossi, we designed a format for teachers to ask questions and give feedback about weekly shared reading. We videotaped Sarah throughout the week as she covered all five days of the weekly shared reading structure, and we shared the tape at the professional development sessions. We devoted the last professional development meeting to planning for weekly shared reading in classrooms. Sarah planned with the fourth and four-five split grades, and Maria guided the third-grade team. Maria also modeled weekly shared reading instruction in third- and fourth-grade classrooms. And everyone agreed to launch weekly shared reading in classrooms the following week.

The upper-grade teachers at PS59 were committed to the idea of planning for and implementing weekly shared reading in their classrooms, partly because they philosophically agreed with it, and partly because they too shaped and constructed the idea.

# The Power of Reflection—Once Again

After the first week of the upper-grade implementation of weekly shared reading, we invited reflection and feedback from the teachers. Again, taking time to reflect on our practices was crucial to the sustainability and purpose of weekly shared reading at PS59. Because we were committed to the idea of weekly shared reading, we set aside time weekly for teachers to reflect on their instruction and plan for the upcoming week's text. Barbara Rossi and Wendy Binkowitz, our third-grade colleagues, and Maria met every Friday afternoon to consider the teaching and learning from the past week and to make plans for the following week. Based on our reflections during our third-grade conversations, we tweaked the teaching points, added more nonfiction texts, used colored copies to further engage our students, and introduced English language arts test passages to our third graders for the first time.

And one night, a few months after the upper-grade adoption of weekly shared reading, the upper-grade teachers and leadership team received the following email from Barbara Rossi:

> Date: Mar 6, 2005 3:35 P.M.
> Subject: Shared Reading Epiphany
>
> Hello All,
>
> I know after you read this email, you are going to think I am crazy but I had this positive thought and I had to share it!

I was sitting in some meeting this week and I was thinking about shared reading. I was thinking about how it has opened new doors to my teaching. This week I taught a social studies lesson on Australia using a Let's Go Time for Kids. Thursday morning I ran to Staples for my color overhead copies. (They now recognize me at the copy counter!) I was so excited to teach this lesson. I made copies of the feature cover, the fun map of Australia and a page of postcards. During Social Studies the kids were so excited to talk about the Koala cover and the map of Australia. I felt like I had done all this explicit teaching around the features of this magazine before I sent them off to work independently. Instead of the kids rushing through the magazine they really seemed interested in reading it thoroughly.

Last year, before our shared reading initiative, I would never have thought about spending as much time unpacking the text and really studying it together.

Anyway that's my epiphany. I just wanted to share this light bulb that went off in my mind. I also wanted to thank everyone for their shared reading support. I think our reading instruction has gotten so much better this year and it's exciting to be a part of this growth at P.S. 59.

Best,
Barbara

The learning community at PS59, strengthened by work of the Teachers College Reading and Writing Project, led by smart instructional leaders, and supported by dynamic teachers, implemented an upper-grade initiative that transformed our teaching and students' learning. The following school year, our leadership team and the upper-grade teachers explicitly stated that weekly shared reading was to be taught in grades three though five; it became an instructional practice a year after inception.

# Our Kids

Weekly shared reading changed the instructional practices of the teachers at PS59. We would be remiss, however, if we did not celebrate the transformation of our learners. While the teaching staff created new thinking through an exciting schoolwide initiative, our students grew their thinking through the five essential reading skills, exposure to various genres, and opportunities for partnership and whole-group conversations.

Throughout the book, we've shared snapshots of students who were impacted by the tight and purposeful instruction in weekly shared reading. Both readers who excelled and readers who struggled were often pushed further through questioning, conversation, and prompting on our part as practitioners. Weekly shared reading was one more chance for readers to read during their school day, and one more chance for us to teach our students the habits and skills of proficient readers.

Weekly shared reading became such an ingrained part of our upper-grade curriculum that we relied on it to introduce our students to genres or ideas, reteach a concept or strategy, and highlight an essential reading skill. With minimum time, we maximized reading instruction and further pushed our readers to proficiency.

# Final Thoughts

The power of weekly shared reading evolves through tailored, assessment-driven instruction, delivered in clips of ten to fifteen minutes throughout the week. It's powerful for teachers because they have multiple opportunities to assess students, to more efficiently meet the needs in their classroom, and to nip issues of comprehension breakdown before they grow larger. It's powerful for the students—the budding readers—because they play the part of the proficient reader, move into a world of literacy, and familiarize themselves with texts of various genres. This symbiotic relationship between teacher and student—between fluent reader and growing reader—is strengthened during weekly shared reading sessions, as we make meaning of a text together.

Weekly shared reading allows for access to more sophisticated texts in a highly scaffolded instructional approach. It is the "with" phase in the gradual release of responsibility—the time to support students as they take on more challenging work, as they push themselves as readers. Our students' reading becomes visible and we guide them to a deeper analysis and understanding of various texts.

So invite your students into a world of literacy. Allow them to feel what it feels like to be a most proficient reader. Provide the melody from the words on the page, and work through comprehending the text together. Push your readers—help them to grow in their skill development, show them strategies to access and understand texts, and encourage them to linger with literature. And as you cultivate a group of readers, you will also cultivate a supportive, learning community, where readers can safely take risks, express their thinking, and build ideas together.

# Appendix

# A Sampling of Texts* Used During Weekly Shared Reading

## Poetry

Dakos, Kalli. 1995. "Call the Periods Call the Commas." *If You're Not Here, Please Raise Your Hand: Poems About School.* New York: Aladdin.

Fleischman, Paul. 1988. *Joyful Noise: Poems for Two Voices.* New York: HarperTrophy.

Greenfield, Eloise. 1978. *Honey, I Love.* New York: HarperCollins.

Livingston, Myra Cohn. 1994. "Quiet." Ed. Lee Bennett Hopkins. *April Bubbles Chocolate.* New York: Simon & Schuster.

McLoughland, Beverly. 1990. "Surprise." Ed. Lee Bennett Hopkins. *Good Books, Good Times!* New York: HarperCollins.

Merriam, Eve. 2006. "How to Eat a Poem." Ed. American Poetry and Literacy Project. *How to Eat a Poem: A Smorgasbord of Tasty and Delicious Poems for Young Readers.* Mineola, NY: Dover.

Schenk de Regniers, Beatrice. 2005. "Keep a Poem in Your Pocket." Ed. Caroline Kennedy. *A Family of Poems: My Favorite Poetry for Children.* New York: Hyperion.

Worth, Valerie. 1994. *All the Small Poems and Fourteen More.* New York: Farrar, Straus, and Giroux.

## Nonfiction

Davis, Kenneth C. 2003. *Don't Know Much About History: Everything You Need to Know About American History but Never Learned.* New York: HarperCollins.

Dubowski, Cathy East. 1998. *Shark Attack!* New York: DK Publishing, Inc.

Marshall, Sally. 2005. "A Childhood Without Crickets Isn't So Bad." *Newsweek* March 28. (May also be found at www.newsweek.com.)

Mathematics Advantage, New York Grade 5 (practice test).

---

*With the chapter books, I just pick out one section or one page.

New York State Testing Program. 2005. Grade 3: Mathematics. Book 2. Sample
     Test. New York: McGraw-Hill. www.emsc.nysed.gov/3-8/math-sample/
     home.htm.
Polin, C. J. 2005. *The Story of Chocolate*. New York: DK.

   fliers

   graphs

   interviews

   *Kids Discover* articles

   menus

   *Time for Kids* articles

   time lines

Stanley, Jerry. 1992. "Black Blizzard." *Scholastic Scope* v46.

## Fiction

Bunting, Eve. 1991. *Fly Away Home*. New York: Clarion.

Cleary, Beverly. 1981. *Ramona Quimby, Age 8*. New York: HarperCollins.

Cooney, Barbara. 1982. *Miss Rumphius*. New York: Viking Penguin.

Crews, Donald. 1992. *Shortcut*. New York: Greenwillow.

dePaola, Tomie. 1979. *Oliver Button Is a Sissy*. Orlando, FL: Voyager.

Gregory, Kristiana. 2002. *We Are Patriots: Hope's Revolutionary War Diary*.
     New York: Scholastic.

Griffin, Judith Berry. 1977. *Phoebe the Spy*. New York: Coward, McCann, and
     Geoghegan.

Little, Jean. 1986. *Hey World, Here I Am!* Toronto: Kids Can.

Rylant, Cynthia. 1982. *When I Was Young in the Mountains*. Boston: E. P.
     Dutton.

———. 1985. "Spaghetti." *Every Living Thing*. New York: Simon & Schuster.

———. 1987. *Henry and Mudge*. New York: Simon and Schuster.

———. 1997. *Poppleton and Friends*. New York: Scholastic.

Sharma, Marjorie Weinman. 1977. *Nate the Great*. New York: Yearling.

Woodson, Jacqueline. 2001. *The Other Side*. New York: G. P. Putnam's Sons.

# References

Allington, Richard. 2000. *What Really Matters for Struggling Readers: Designing Research-Based Programs.* Columbus, OH: Allyn & Bacon.

Bakhtin, Mikhail. 1982. *The Dialogic Imagination: Four Essays.* Ed. Michael Holquist; trans. Caryn Emerson and Michael Holquist. Austin: University of Texas Press.

Bloom, Benjamin, S., ed. 1956. *Taxonomy of Educational Objectives: Handbook 1. Cognitive Domain.* New York: Longman.

Bomer, Randy. 2003. "Minds on Fire: Teaching Readers to Think as They Read." Paper presented at Teachers College, New York, October.

Brown, Sue. 2004. *Shared Reading for Grades 3 and Beyond: Working It Out Together.* Wellington, New Zealand: Learning Media.

Buchanan Smith, Doris. 1973. *A Taste of Blackberries.* New York: HarperCollins.

Bunting, Eve. 1991. *Fly Away Home.* New York: Clarion.

Calkins, Lucy, Kate Montgomery, and Donna Santman, with Beverly Falk. 1998. *A Teacher's Guide to Standarized Reading Tests: Knowledge Is Power.* Portsmouth, NH: Heinemann.

Cambourne, Brian. 1988. *The Whole Story: Natural Learning and the Acquisition of Literacy in the Classroom.* Auckland, Australia: Ashton Scholastic.

Casey, Katherine. 2006. *Literacy Coaching: The Essentials.* Portsmouth, NH: Heinemann.

Cunningham, Patricia, and Richard Allington. 1994. *Classrooms That Work: They Can ALL Read and Write.* Boston: Pearson Education.

dePaola, Tomie. 1979. *Oliver Button Is a Sissy.* New York: Voyager Harcourt Brace.

Fosnot, Catherine Twomey, and Maarten Dolk. 2001. *Young Mathematicians at Work: Constructing Number Sense, Addition, and Subtraction.* Portsmouth, NH: Heinemann.

Frey, James. 2003. *A Million Little Pieces.* New York: Doubleday, Nan A. Talese.

Gallas, Karen. 1995. *Talking Their Way into Science: Hearing Children's Questions and Theories, Responding with Curricula.* New York: Teachers College Press.

Gregory, Kristiana. 2002. *We Are Patriots: Hope's Revolutionary Diary.* New York: Scholastic.

Harvey, Stephanie, and Anne Goudvis. 2000. *Strategies That Work: Teaching Comprehension to Enhance Understanding.* Portland, ME: Stenhouse.

Heard, Georgia. 1999. *Awakening the Heart: Exploring Poetry in Elementary and Middle School.* Portsmouth, NH: Heinemann.

Hiassen, Carl. 2002. *Hoot.* New York: Knopf Books for Young Readers.

Holdaway, Don. 1980. *Independence in Reading: A Handbook on Individualized Procedures.* Gosford, Australia: Ashton Scholastic.

Keene, Ellin Oliver, and Susan Zimmermann. 1997. *Mosaic of Thought: Teaching Comprehension in a Reader's Workshop.* Portsmouth, NH: Heinemann.

Lareau, Annette. 2003. *Unequal Childhoods: Class, Race, and Family Life.* California: University of California Press.

LeBlanc, Adrian Nicole. 2003. *Random Family: Love, Drugs, Trouble, and Coming of Age in the Bronx.* New York: Scribner.

New York State Testing Program. 2005. Grade 3: Mathematics. Book 2. Sample Test. New York: McGraw-Hill. www.emsc.nysed.gov/3-8/math-sample/home.htm.

Parkes, Brenda. 2000. *Read It Again! Revisiting Shared Reading.* Portland, ME: Stenhouse.

Paterson, Katherine. 1979. *Bridge to Terabithia.* New York: Crowell.

Pearson, P. David, and M. C. Gallagher. 1983. "The Instruction of Reading Comprehension." *Contemporary Educational Psychology* 8: 317–44.

Routman, Regie. 2000. *Conversations: Strategies for Teaching, Learning, and Evaluating.* Portsmouth, NH: Heinemann.

Rylant, Cynthia. 1985. "Spaghetti." *Every Living Thing.* New York: Simon & Schuster.

Sachar, Louis. 1998. *Holes.* New York: Dell Yearling.

Satterfield, Kathryn. 2006. "An Immigrant Nation." *Time for Kids*, April 7. (May also be found at www.timeforkids.com.)

Schenk de Regniers, Beatrice. 2005. "Keep a Poem in Your Pocket." Ed. Caroline Kennedy. *A Family of Poems: My Favorite Poetry for Children.* New York: Hyperion.

Scieszka, Jon. 1991. *Time Warp Trio.* New York: Puffin, Penguin.

Sharmat, Marjorie Weinman. 1972–2006. Nate the Great series. New York: Random House.

Smith, Betty. 1993. *A Tree Grows in Brooklyn.* New York, London: Harper and Brothers.

Snicket, Lemony. 1999–2006. A Series of Unfortunate Events. New York: HarperCollins Children's.

Stewart, Sharon. 2004. *It's a Mammal!* Melbourne, Australia: Pearson Education.

Woodson, Jacqueline. 2001. *The Other Side.* New York: Putnam.

Zimmermann, Susan, and Chryse Hutchins. 2003. *7 Keys to Comprehension: How to Help Your Kids Read It and Get It!* New York: Three Rivers.